Surprising Ways
God Answers Prayer

KAREN BARBER

SPIRE

© 2001 by Karen Barber

Published by Fleming H. Revell
a division of Baker Publishing Group
P.O. Box 6287, Grand Rapids, MI 49516-6287
www.revellbooks.com

Spire edition published 2006
ISBN 10: 0-8007-8746-3
ISBN 978-0-8007-8746-2

Paperback edition published in 2004 under the title *Surprised by Prayer: The Wonderful Ways God Answers*

Previously published in 2001 under the title *Surprised by Prayer!: The Joyous, Unexpected Ways God Answers Your Needs* by Guideposts

Printed in the United States of America

This book is dedicated to those who have allowed me to share their wonderful stories of answered prayer. It has been a privilege to know each one of you, to be able to hear first-hand such remarkable stories, to be granted the opportunity to ask all sorts of questions, and to receive such thoughtful, illuminating replies. Thank you for opening your hearts and lives to me. You have helped my prayers become more courageous.

CONTENTS

ACKNOWLEDGMENTS

I would like to thank the following people who helped in the creation of this book: Terri Castillo, Brigitte Weeks, and Elizabeth Kramer Gold.

Eternal thanks go to Lonnie Hull DuPont for her impeccable editing job on this book, her expansive heart, and her keen wisdom. What an amazing answer to prayer to be assigned such a gifted editor.

I would also like to express my appreciation for those who have helped me develop my skills as a writer. I am particularly indebted to the *Guideposts* workshopper system that trains writers and to Jim McDermott who has so ably led us. Thank you, Jim, for your cheerful way of teaching us so many valuable lessons on how to write a solid, entertaining story that points up spiritual truths. Your work sets the standard for everything a writer needs and hopes for in an editor.

I would also like to acknowledge Stephanie Vink, Karen Steele, and the Revell editorial and marketing team for their expertise and support in presenting this work to potential readers. May God bless each and every one of you.

1

SURPRISED
BY PRAYER

*I lay my requests before you and
wait in expectation.*

Psalm 5:3

On Sunday, September 13, I was not simply surprised by prayer, I was utterly astounded. As I neared my mother's room on the neurology hall in the hospital, I nearly collided with a nurse and a bearded doctor rushing into Mom's room. *Oh, no,* I thought fearfully.

I stood there unable to go in, as if someone had bolted my feet to the floor in the doorway. Dad saw me and jumped up out of his chair at Mom's bedside. He hurried over, grabbed my arm and exclaimed, "Susie opened her eyes when the preacher was here!"

I could not answer, I was so astonished. On Tuesday night, Mom had been stricken with a massive brain stem stroke. The only hopeful sign was on the first day, when Mom had seemed to slightly move the toes on her left foot in response to a therapist. Since then she had failed to show any sign of conscious life, not even when a flashlight was beamed directly into her propped-open eye, not even when she was stuck with a needle. In accordance with Mom's living will, we disconnected all life support, expecting her to die.

The brisk squeak as the nurse flung aside the curtain that surrounded Mom's bed told me that I was not just imagining things. The doctor leaned over Mom's still form and called loudly, "Mrs. Brown! Mrs. Brown!"

A small ripple of animation stirred on Mom's face, something like pea gravel being dropped into a child's water-filled beach bucket. Slowly, as if being abruptly awakened from a peaceful dream, Mom's hazy blue eyes fluttered open and gave the doctor a startled look.

The doctor wheeled around and barked to the nurse, "We need to start treating her more aggressively!"

As the doctor and nurse rushed out into the corridor, we crowded around Mom's bedside, trying to think what we should say. Dad finally crowed, "Hey Susie, can you wiggle your toes for us?"

I teased back before Dad undid the bed sheets, "Dad, how about if we take off *your* shoes and tickle *your* feet?"

Mom's face crept into a half smile that made an amused lump on her good left side and fell loosely aside on the right. Mom had not only heard, she had understood us. She was still wondrously alive, still with us on this earth, and still smiling crookedly about the blessed oddity of it all.

I was dazed when I telephoned Aunt Josie. Her voice rose in jubilation as she croaked, "Praise God! It's an answer to prayer! The whole church prayed for Susie this morning."

As I hung up, I was glad someone was doing a jig, because I was still in shock. But I knew with certainty that this breakthrough was indeed orchestrated by a power far beyond human scope and eons ahead of modern medicine. Even in my wildest dreams, I had not imagined that Mom would revive.

Should We Be Surprised?

After standing next to my mother when she suddenly startled back to conscious life that Sunday afternoon, I have since wondered about my dumbfounded response. Should I have been so shocked? After all, I had been a member of countless prayer groups, prayer chains, and prayer partnerships, and I had attended prayer classes and seminars of every sort. Years earlier I had even attempted writing a book on prayer. More to the point, I had been praying for Mom for six full days. Yet I had been just as utterly astonished at seeing Mom's eyes flutter open as Mom had been at the sight of the doctor's bearded face hanging over her, braying out her name.

At first, connecting the words *surprise* and *prayer* seems contradictory. The very fact that we pray at all demonstrates faith in a loving Creator who continues to act and care for his creation. Faith would seem to intimate that there should be no surprise whatsoever when prayers are answered.

But joining surprise and prayer makes absolute sense when our astonishment stems not from the simple fact that our prayers are answered, but rather from the unlikely ways and means through which the answers dawn upon us. Surprise requires anticipation. I assumed that my mother was terminally stricken. I assumed that she would never smile or speak again. Thankfully, my assumptions were quite wrong, and the surprise was on me.

Anticipation is one of God's gifts to us. We need powerful abilities of projection to prepare ourselves physically and psychologically for coming events. At the same time, God also tells us to pray, to bring our needs before him in recognition of our limitations against the unseen forces that move the universe. The God who put us together understands that as we pray, we will envision the most likely way things might turn out, even though it often means applying simplistic logic to complicated situations or superimposing limited experience onto one-of-a-kind happenings. We are, in effect, masters at setting ourselves up for surprise.

Far from being a curse, our mismatched abilities to antici- pate and to pray are the divine ingredients for a marvelous and holy gift—the ability to apprehend and enjoy moments of awestruck wonder. These other-earthly moments are none other than the divine shiver that rekindles our awareness of the touchable nearness of a loving God ever moving on the quiet currents of prayer.

To research this book, I had to readjust my view of prayer. In the past I had focused on saying the right words (Heal my mother—if it be Thy will), developing the right theological attitudes (Do I have enough faith to ask this?), and applying the right disciplines (Did I remember to pray before driving to the hospital?). I was so concerned with the mechanics of praying that I had failed to ask myself, "Have I developed the ability to discover an answer, however unlikely, to every prayer?"

Perhaps those of us who have studied and practiced prayer have never stopped to consider that seeing the answers to prayer is a skill that might be developed and improved. Yet I dare say none of us would want to miss any of God's answers.

I have a suspicion that part of our problem lies in our assumption that prayer answers come in only one size.

Big and Dramatic Answers

The story of my mother's deathbed reawakening is exactly the sort of testimony of answered prayer we customarily hear reported and repeated. Interestingly enough, my mother's reawakening is the only such "miraculous answer" I have witnessed firsthand in over forty years of praying. Although I have interviewed countless people with amazing stories of rescue and survival to tell, as far as the hands-on experience of my own ordinary life, such astounding answers have been rare. I have found that the big and dramatic answers are the exception, and small, daily "miracles" are more the rule.

Instead of enjoying the God-glorifying marvel of the big and dramatic answers and then going happily on with the equally fascinating rest of our lives, we have a tendency to keep staring back at the spectacular answers as if they were the only show in town. In so doing, we are like people looking directly into the sun. Unfortunately, when we look back at the normal things about us, we cannot see beyond the large spots still burned in our eyes. No wonder we might miss the other more plentiful answers that have quietly dawned upon the scene with a more subtle heavenly gleam.

Fragile Moments

The most easily missed prayer answers are fragile moments when nothing monumental happens. Once we finally glimpse the divine undercurrent, we are enveloped with a different kind of awe—more like a soft blanket of peace than a blazing fire of astonishment. The true miracle of such moments is that we sense the brush of God's fingertips at all. The fragility of such moments is not only in the seeing but in the retelling. How difficult to communicate a heart strangely stirred to someone who did not experience that brief breath of divinity. Because of our inability to describe such moments in words, we seldom share them as answers to prayer in public gatherings. Therefore, we overlook and discount them. Their delicate nature leaves it squarely up to us to treasure and store these fragile moments in our hearts, welcoming them as no less legitimate answers to prayer than miraculous happenings that can be enthusiastically proclaimed from the rooftop.

Such a fragile moment occurred the autumn following Mom's stroke. Mom's recovery had been earned through determination, therapy, and Dad's constant care. I worried about the terrible burdens of wheelchairs, adult diapers, and cooking meals that Dad was coping with, and I prayed that their two-day visit in our home would be a time of rest and renewal for him. My prayer seemed to evaporate into wishful thinking as I helped Dad haul in all of the paraphernalia they needed. Then there was the knock on my bedroom door for help in the middle of the night; Mom had fallen out of bed because there were no safety rails on the guest bed.

The following day, just when I had nearly lost all hope that my prayer would be answered, the afternoon sun came out, and Dad suggested we sit on our back deck. As we settled into plastic chairs, Dad remarked, "Isn't this delightful?" There was a branch of brilliant red leaves near the deck, and after a while Dad said, "Do you see that, Susie? Isn't that pretty. I wonder if that's a dogwood."

Mom nodded, "Yes, it's probably a dogwood."

Quite satisfied, Dad leaned back and repeated, "Isn't this absolutely delightful."

I looked at his nodding head and realized that this repetition was no accident. His face showed that he could not have been more rejuvenated if he had been sitting on the deck chair of a cruise ship on a sparkling emerald sea. God had not dramatically lifted Dad's daily burdens, but rather was stirring within my father a different grace—the ability to find joy and pleasure in the smallest of things—warm sunshine, a flaming red leaf—and the simple fact that Mom could answer. God was there in that moment, magnificently whispering through a simple combination of light, warmth, color, and shared companionship. There was no event to report, simply everything to be felt.

That evening when my husband Gordon came home for dinner, he asked, "So what did you do today?"

Suddenly it seemed a bit ridiculous to say, "Well, we sat on the deck in the sunshine and saw some red leaves and Dad liked it and God was there." Instead I replied, "Oh, we didn't do much of anything," unable to put the nearly missed moment of nearness to God into adequate words.

Right before Our Eyes

Other times we miss prayer answers because they have been right before our eyes all along. At first and even second glance, the answer seems too ordinary to be even remotely divine. One example is shoes. Jim Neal, a forester from Newberry, South Carolina, wears size fifteen-D shoes. But his shoes were the farthest thing from Jim's mind when he prayed, "Lord, use me to spread the gospel."

Jim jumped at the chance to help at a conference in Amsterdam for itinerant evangelists from all over the world. Unfortunately, Jim's most glamorous assignment was to punch the on button for a video about finances. Frustrated with his lack of "ministry," Jim left his post as soon as he could and took a shortcut through an alleyway that looked like it would lead back to his hotel. There he happened upon a queue of evangelists in front of a door marked "Samaritan's Purse," waiting to select donated clothing to take back to their families.

Jim was wearing a pair of special-order blue athletic shoes, and he thought, What if there's a man here with size fifteen feet wearing hand-me-down size thirteen shoes? Impulsively he sang out, "Who has the biggest feet?"

Those who understood English mobbed him as the line disintegrated into a jostling, good-natured, foot-comparing contest. Foot after foot continued to miss the size of Jim's huge shoe by at least five inches.

Suddenly a hand gripped Jim's shoulder. "Papa, I can wear those shoes."

Jim turned to view the foot of the intercessor and did not think for a minute he was looking at a size fifteen. The rotund African man's foot was not big; it was, instead, hard to fit—with an arch so painfully high that the man could not lace his shoes. Instead, he was forced to leave the leather tongue lolling.

Jim protested, "My shoe won't fit you," but the evangelist had already pulled off his right shoe. Jim doubtfully surrendered his own right shoe, and the man eagerly tried it on, exclaiming, "Oh, this is good! I can tie them!"

"But your foot ends two inches before the shoe."

"It's all right," the man insisted, "I can stuff paper in them."

Against his better judgment, Jim promised the man his shoes, agreeing to give them to him that evening when he could change into his loafers. That night when the evangelist spied Jim, the man sat right down on the hotel lobby floor and put on the huge blue athletic shoes with the gray racing stripe down the side, never minding he was dressed in a black suit, white dress shirt and a tie. As the beaming evangelist left, one of Jim's friends remarked, "That man looked like a duck waddling out of here in those shoes."

In January, Jim received a letter from Nigeria: "I wear your shoes every day and thank the Lord for you. People stop and stare at my shoes wherever I go and they want to know how I got them. No one here has ever seen such big shoes. I stop and talk to them about Jesus."

Jim put down the note, and looked down at his feet in astonishment. All along, Jim had been expecting God to use his voice to evangelize. Instead, God had led him down an alleyway in Amsterdam to give away his shoes to a man who lived thousands of miles away in Africa, where his sideshow shoes would themselves become "Good News shoes."

Mysterious Circumstances

Up until a few years ago, this category of prayer answers was rarely mentioned in traditional circles. Few shared see-ing a mysterious light, hearing an insistent voice that led to safety, finding an object that was not there even a mo-ment earlier, being helped by an ordinary enough person who later vanished. Fortunately, the growing popularity of angel stories has opened us up to seeing and sharing such mysterious answers to prayer.

To ignore this type of answer to prayer would cause us to throw out whole sections of the Bible. We remember that God spoke directly to Abraham, one of the giants of the faith. God even sent angels to visit him (Gen. 18:1–15). But do we recall that ordinary folks in the Bible experienced the same thing? For instance, Sarah's slave girl Hagar runs away from her mistress and is astonished to hear an angel say, "Hagar, servant of Sarah, where have you come from and where are you going?" (Gen. 16:8). So sure that she has indeed heard from God, Hagar returns to her mistress with a new name for God that was singularly personal and powerful for the ancient and barbaric times in which she lived. Her name for God? "You are the God who sees me" (Gen. 16:13).

Tootie McElhannon, of Conyers, Georgia, encountered an answer from the God who not only sees us but knows us the day her thirteen-year-son Joel was nearly killed. In the days before bicycle helmets, Joel was cycling down a hill in the neighborhood when he missed a stop sign. A car turning the corner hit Joel's bicycle head-on. Joel's head smashed the car's windshield, his body was catapulted over the top of the car, his rear end hit the trunk of the car, and he was thrown to the pavement.

Tootie arrived just as the ambulance did, praying, "Lord help us!" As a large crowd of horrified neighbors and witnesses gathered, Tootie, who is a nurse, began reviewing all of the possible injuries. Unfortunately, her medical knowledge made her become more hysterical by the moment.

Just then a white-haired gentleman walking a large black dog came up to Tootie. "I'm a doctor," he said. Without so much as laying a hand on Joel, the man started at the top of Joel's head and began describing what was wrong with him and what was not. "These are just superficial cuts here, there's no concussion, there are no broken bones here." As the man finished his assessment, Tootie calmed down. Then the man opened the ambulance door and helped her in.

At the hospital, all of the white-haired doctor's observations turned out to be correct. Joel was bruised and banged up, but otherwise sound. The next day as neighbors called to inquire about Joel, Tootie began asking about the white-haired gentleman in hopes of thanking him. To a person, each neighbor declared that no such man lived in the neighborhood. More puzzling still, not one of the witnesses had seen a white-haired man or a big black dog near the ambulance the day before. Baffled, Tootie at last asked Joel if he had seen the elusive man with a black dog at the accident scene. "Of course I saw him," Joel replied, "I passed him at the top of the hill right before I got hit."

Merry Answers

A final category of prayer answers that perhaps has not been greatly explored before is what I call merry answers. Often, I find myself smiling at a highly unlikely or even humorous chain of events that brings about a wonderful resolution to some pesky daily problem. In my view, good-natured laughter should be ringing from the chambers of every prayer meeting as we finally see face-to-face the contrast between our grandiose ideas and our solidly human bumbling. Perhaps in our laughter rings a heavenly note of joyful repentance, for in it we acknowledge our own shortsightedness and God's twenty-twenty vision of our true selves and needs. Sometimes, simply the laughter itself is the breath of grace we needed, offering a small oasis of relief and perspective amidst a tense and uncomfortable situation.

When Jesus says, "With the measure you use, it will be measured to you," we assume he is talking about generosity, reward, or judgment (Mark 4:24). But might it also hint of aptness and poetic justice? Another way of putting it might be, "What you dish out gets dished back to you." Such was the case the day I was dogged by a tag.

On this particular day, I had just jauntily waved good-bye to the former owner of my newly purchased, used minivan. I began backing out of the parking space, but when I went to shift into drive, I mistakenly grabbed the emergency brake. Then I engaged what I thought was the turn signal, and the windshield wipers came on. Nothing's where it should be on this dashboard, I thought. This is the same make as my old van, so why on earth did they have to change everything so I couldn't just sit down here in the driver's seat and be off? What are all of these warning lights and buzzers? I don't like this van one bit. About the only thing that I understood clearly on the new dashboard was the gas gauge, which was sitting on empty.

Later at the gas station, I was complaining to the Lord, "I know we prayed about finding the right car, but this seems like a mistake." No sooner had I finished than my eyes fell upon the crowning blow: a vanity license tag that would have to remain on the car until the title cleared. It proclaimed, "LV2CUT."

Oh, great, I thought, I'm going to be driving around in a car with a tag that says "love to cut." Obviously the former owner was a hairdresser who advertised with her license tag. But what if some driver suffering from road rage thinks "love to cut" means I cut in front of people in traffic?

By the time I arrived home, I was not dwelling on happy and thankful thoughts concerning our new minivan. My sixteen-year-old son, Chris, came out to the garage to look over the new vehicle, and I took the opportunity to complain about everything that I did not like about it. Finally I showed Chris the license tag.

Chris grinned, "Cool. Love to cut. It's just right if you ask me. It goes with our last name. Barber."

It was only then that I realized that God, indeed, had a hand in picking out a car for us, right down to the tag. What was missing in the picture was the thankful recipient. By being a picky grumbler over a perfectly good car, I had dished out absurdity and had been dished back a good laugh by the delightful God who thought up laughter in the first place.

Beginning to See God's Answers

Once we have expanded our idea of the shapes and sizes of prayer answers to include miracles, fragile moments, things right before our eyes, mysterious events, and moments of merry recognition, we are ready to begin matching up answers to our requests. But often we do not know how to go about it. When thinking about prayer answers, we often misconstrue passages such as this one found in Matthew 7:9–11:

> "Which of you, if his son asks for bread, will give him a stone? Or if he asks for a fish, will give him a snake? If you, then, though you are evil, know how to give good gifts to your children, how much more will your Father in heaven give good gifts to those who ask him!"

When we read this, we unconsciously turn the first two verses into formulas instead of suppositions. Using *if-then* logic, this is what we mistakenly read: *if* you ask for bread, *then* you get bread; *if* you ask for a fish, *then* you get a fish. Instead, I think Jesus is saying, "*Suppose* your son asks for bread. Would you give him something inedible? Of course not; you would give him something nourishing."

Once we stop misreading these suppositions, we can lay hold of the *if-then* truth in this passage. "*If* you know how to give good gifts to your children, *then* certainly God knows how on a much larger scale."

Therefore, answers to prayer do not always exactly match our original requests, just as asking for a fish does not always mean getting a fish. Sometimes we get what we wanted. Other times we receive something else just as useful. The Scripture promises that when we ask, we will receive *something* perfectly suited for us from our Father, who knows more than we do what we really need.

21

My friend Charlene Stamper began to discover God's wisdom in answering on March 30, 1980, when she wrote a request in her journal for her four-year-old son. Neal was an active preschooler with curly blond hair and enormous blue eyes. But he suffered from a severe stuttering problem. Charlene was quite worried. Since Neal was unable to answer quickly and could not express himself clearly, she was afraid that he would be labeled a slow learner when he began kindergarten in the fall.

Charlene opened a blank page in her journal and wrote, "I pray that Neal's speech be healed and that his mental and physical capabilities be brought together to make him the perfect little boy of God's design."

When Charlene took Neal to a speech pathologist, the therapist suggested, "Sit down with a tape recorder every day and record the two of you having a normal conversation so he can practice expressing himself."

Charlene says, "I agreed to do it, but I thought what a bother it would be to corral a preschooler every afternoon to sit down for fifteen minutes. My daughter Amy was seven, and I was already very busy running the household. Putting one more thing on the schedule was not my idea of answered prayer. My idea of the way things should work out was that the speech therapist would fix Neal's problems right away."

The following afternoon, Charlene pried Neal away from his toy cars, took him to the screened porch, and got out the tape recorder. As Neal struggled to answer Charlene's questions, the fifteen minutes seemed to drag by.

One day during their session, Neal was paying more attention to the bird hopping across the back lawn than to their conversation. When Neal begged to go out to pet the bird, Charlene said, "You can't pet birds. They fly away." The third time he asked, however, she finally gave in.

Of course, as soon as Neal burst through the screen door and ran toward the bird, it flew off. As Charlene watched her son engaged in that moment of hopeful trying, she thought, *Isn't this the whole point of this practice, to give a chance for Neal to express himself without feeling pressured? I've been so worried he'll still be stuttering when he's seventeen that I haven't let myself enjoy him being four.*

After that, Charlene's attitude toward the sessions began to change. When she asked, "What's our house made out of?" and Neal labored to say, "Brr-i-cckk," she heard more than inarticulate words. She listened in fascination to his thoughts on bricks. Their house was safe because bricks were safe. He based this on the fact that the wolf could not huff and puff and blow down the third little pig's brick house.

Eventually the lessons with the speech therapist were discontinued because of scheduling problems, but Charlene continued her special time with Neal every afternoon. Unfortunately, his speech showed little improvement, and he was still stuttering noticeably when he began kindergarten in September. Then one day in October, Neal came home from school and proclaimed, "See my picture?"

As he handed her the wrinkled paper, Charlene asked, "What did you say?"

"See my picture?" he repeated, enunciating every word correctly as he had the first time.

"That's so wonderful," she said, burying him in a hug. *I've been thinking since he started school that his speech has been improving little by little*, she thought in amazement. *All of a sudden, his stutter is gone.*

The next morning, Charlene thankfully wrote in the margin of her journal next to the prayer request she had written six months earlier, "Neal's speech is healed."

Charlene's story is an example of how asking for a fish does not necessarily equal getting a fish right away. She asked God to heal her son. God did not immediately take away Neal's problems, and surprisingly, that in itself turned out to be a good gift. During that time, God was slowing Charlene down for fifteen minutes a day so that she could rediscover the joy of motherhood.

Three years later when Neal was seven, Charlene was hospitalized with a serious blood infection. Afterward she went into a deep depression. She says, "For six months, I wasn't able to function. I couldn't care for my children or be there for them like I wanted to. I feel that God provided that time on the back porch to strengthen my relationship with Neal for the difficult times ahead."

As Charlene reflected on answered prayer, she went on to tell how Neal helped her further understand God's ways of answering, in a small incident that happened when Neal was six. On Monday, he began talking about the coming weekend, when he and his dad, Ed, were going fishing in a small neighborhood pond. The boy talked earnestly and assuredly about the fish they were going to catch, and, unfortunately, one night during bedtime prayers he asked to catch one on Saturday.

Charlene had no idea if there actually were any fish in the pond, and if there were, would Ed know what sort of bait such fish might strike? Saturday dawned a beautiful day, and the father and son set off on their fishing expedition. While they were gone, Charlene worried about what would happen to Neal's faith if he did not get a fish. She prayed, "God, please let him at least catch one fish—even a small one."

When Charlene finally saw Neal coming up the driveway, he was grinning from ear to ear, holding a brown, wet fish about four inches long by the tail. "Look at what we got!" he called out.

But the closer Neal got, the odder the fish seemed. It was not rubbery but appeared rather stiff as he swung it. And it was not shiny but dull. In fact, it looked like it was covered in mud. Finally, he was close enough for Charlene to see the truth. Neal's "fish" was not a fish at all, but rather a flat rock shaped just like a fish. He said, "I looked down and there this was by the pond. Mom, I told you we'd get a fish."

Charlene affirmed, "Isn't that a wonderful answer to prayer?"

"Yep," he nodded.

Then they all went inside, laughing and smiling.

Today an unusual trophy sits on the bookshelf in Charlene's family room: a plaque with a four-inch rock shaped like a fish glued to it. The fish is there as a reminder that God sometimes answers prayers in ways we do not expect.

In the same way Jesus startled his listeners with the mental picture of biting into a rock instead of bread or frying a scorpion instead of a fish, Charlene was surprised by the rock fish. Such mismatches and ironies invite us to carefully consider his Word until the true meaning sinks in. When Jesus says, "Which of you, if his son asks for bread will give him a stone?" he wants us to understand that the father not only hears the child's request but also sees the hunger behind the request (Matt. 7:9).

When Neal prayed for a fish, he was not looking for food; he was looking to have an adventure. Finding a fish-shaped rock worked splendidly because it met that need. Even though it was a different sort of answer than Charlene expected, it was a much better answer. A fish from the pond would have provided nothing but a small side dish to a long forgotten meal. But a rock fish could remain a feast to the eyes for years to come.

The rock fish, chiseled by God over countless spring thaws, might still be in a weed patch beside the pond today if it had not been for Neal's receptive eyes and heart. He wanted a fish and he was open to anything that might be perceived as fishlike, even if it happened to be inanimate and did not come attached to the end of a hook.

Until that breakthrough moment when we are able to at last see fishlikeness in unexpected places, we will never be surprised by prayer. In fact, we are guaranteed to be routinely disappointed by prayer.

Seeing prayer answers, then, is not a science, but rather an artful way of living. It requires much more of us than knowledge of formulas and principles, education, and physical perception. Seeing prayer answers instead requires sensitivity, creativity, expectancy, curiosity, patience, and that all-important aptitude of perceiving fishlikeness. Jesus says, "For this people's heart has become calloused; they hardly hear with their ears, and they have closed their eyes. Otherwise they might see with their eyes, hear with their ears, understand with their hearts and turn, and I would heal them" (Matt. 13:15). According to this verse, faith grows with each new perception and shrivels and dies with each failure to see. Therefore, our skill at seeing prayer answers is not simply an idle academic pursuit but rather the very doorway to a deeper, richer faith.

Ready to Be Surprised

Learning to see prayer answers is best taught by those who themselves have learned through experience. Therefore, we will approach our subject by investigating true stories of answered prayer that will enable us to think more deeply about our own lives. The stories recounted in this book are about ordinary people whose prayers have been answered in unexpected ways. These accounts are drawn from my own journals and countless interviews and conversations with others. For the sake of authenticity, none of these accounts are secondhand stories from other sources, such as

other books or sermons. As an investigator, I have personally spoken directly to each and every person whose story
is included in this book.

My sole requirement in listing an experience in these
pages was that the person simply asked God to help them
in some way. We will not focus on the quality of the prayers
nor on the virtues of the person who uttered them because,
as mentioned earlier, this is not intended to be a book on how
to pray. Other books on prayer rightly focus on the various
components of prayer, such as praise, thanksgiving, worship,
meditation, confession, and petition. This investigation will
focus solely on petition. What did the person ask for and what
was later given? So this book is not about how to go about
praying, but rather how to go about perceiving and receiving, about how to live our lives with wide-eyed wonder. It
is about limbering up our faith to seek and eventually find
answers to each and every prayer.

There are, of course, many ways in which we are often
surprised by prayer. We will explore our subject by organizing
these true accounts under these general headings: surprised
by unlikely means, by presence, by a word, by a call to pray,
by a partnership, by Scripture, and, finally, by power.

Researching this book has revolutionized my prayer life
by opening my eyes to so many quiet acts of God that I have
so easily overlooked in the past. God's deeds were always
there. My comprehension of them was all that was lacking.
I invite you to meet the people I have met and consider their
powerful stories. In the end, I believe that we shall all learn
to be wonderfully surprised by prayer.

2

SURPRISED
BY UNLIKELY MEANS

Then Moses cried out to the Lord,
and the Lord showed him a piece of
wood. He threw it into the water,
and the water became sweet.

Exodus 15:25

I climbed the three steps leading from the street onto the first-floor porch of the Charleston, South Carolina, house with the characteristic upstairs and downstairs porches running perpendicular to the street. Eighty-two-year-old Mary Mack Brown greeted me through a flimsy screen door, perched in her motorized wheelchair. The house, built in the nineteenth century, was already old when Mary Mack's father purchased it in 1940. She had seen to the rearing of a succession of nieces and nephews and their children in the venerable old house, and Mary Mack herself had grown old under the narrow tin roof. Living independently in her beloved house that held so many powerful memories was certainly not happenstance. "It was a direct answer to prayer," she declared. "Prayer and poodle dogs."

Mary Mack's rich prayer life was no mystery. Right in the middle of telling me about a disagreement with a relative over a box of dishes, she planted her elbows on the wheelchair armrests and spread her hands like palmetto fronds. Then she rolled back her head, pinned her eyes on the tiles tacked to the ceiling, and left off conversing with me and commenced talking with the Lord. "God!" she said with emotion. "You know what I been through. Please lift it off me! I'm going to do my part, and I know you're going to do yours!" Just as seamlessly, her chin fell, the loosened skin draping down like a wrinkled muslin sheet, and she resumed our conversation, telling me of her miraculous rehabilitation at age seventy-five following her first stroke.

"I had my stroke and this whole left side was gone. I couldn't walk and I couldn't move my arm, and the doctors said I wasn't going to get over it. My two sisters were living then, Lee and Lucille, both nurses in New York City. One would come down to stay with me a week, then the other one would come. One day they said, 'Mary Mack, we're going to pack you up and take you to New York where we can take care of you.' I cried like a baby because I didn't want to leave here. Then I prayed to the Lord that somehow, some way, he'd get me well enough to come back home.

"One sister worked at night, and one sister worked during the day. The one who worked during the day got me up in the morning and sat me on the couch in front of the TV

30

until my other sister got home a few hours later. They always had poodle dogs, and there I was—sitting all by myself, and I couldn't even get up—and those poodle dogs would jump up on the sofa.

"All propped up there, I kept praying, 'They taught me a long time ago that man's extremity is God's opportunity. Well, man has done all he knows to do for me. If it's possible and if it's thy will, make a way for me to use this arm and this side again so I can go back home.'

"I sat there for two months, all crippled up and not getting any better. Then one day those poodle dogs—I don't remember their names—jumped up on the sofa like usual. The white one was on my good right side, and the black one on my bad left side. I could use that right hand, so I just sat there patting that white poodle dog and the black poodle dog started getting jealous because he didn't understand why I wasn't patting him, too.

"Well, that black poodle dog started to move around all restless, and finally he just took his head and pushed it right under my left arm and knocked my arm up in the air. I heard something that sounded like a pop, and when my arm came down, I felt the life come back into it and I could use this arm again.

"When my sisters came home, they saw me moving that arm, and they couldn't believe it. Lucille started taking me around to the mall and walking me around, and soon enough they were able to put me on a plane for home. I've been living in my own house ever since."

Mary Mack leaned back in her wheelchair, satisfaction etched on the lines of her face. Then she nonchalantly dropped a benediction that made my jaw drop. "That poodle dog answered more than one of my prayers," she concluded. "You see, because of that poodle dog curing up my arm, my sixty-five-year-old baby sister Lucille finally became a believer."

God's Astonishing Ways and Means

Mary Mack is the perfect person to introduce us to the idea of unlikely ways and means because she herself is one of God's own originals, a powerhouse of faith and pluck disguised by a feeble-looking body. Looks and expectations can be deceiving. If God had transported us to that New York apartment where Mary Mack sat helplessly on the sofa and had asked us to come up with a rehabilitation plan, I am sure that the jealous poodle scenario would not have entered our wildest imaginings. And what about the conversion of Lucille? Who among us would have entrusted that moment of eternal decision to Lucille's own rambunctious pet?

As we discovered in chapter 1, when we pray, we unwittingly set ourselves on a mental collision course by predicting the next turn of events based on the last turn of events. We expect help from a long list of sources of past help: the laws of nature, regular paychecks, modern gizmos, elbow grease, the support of friends and family, and self-help information. Unfortunately, our expectations keep our faith bundled up in this safe, cozy cocoon. We see gray light through our thin paper walls, never guessing that there is a vast and glorious blue sky outside. We expend our energies looking for answers in cramped, probable places, while an ever-changing Providence is moving the constellations at dizzying speeds and swirling clouds at a moment's whimsy into mountains, canyons, and prairie rose gardens.

Unlikely means do not merely solve practical problems in clever or unpredictable ways. Unlikely ways and means move us toward a deeper and more startling faith as they shake us up in the jigger of possibilities. The more we welcome and embrace unlikely means, the more open we will become to *using* unlikely means when God's still small voice suggests a radical but divine course of action. An astounding example in the Bible is Joshua and the Battle of Jericho. Only a man inspired by God—or a madman—would have employed the strategy of marching around the walls of the impregnable city once a day for six days and then on the seventh day, marching around seven times while blowing trumpets (Joshua 6). Strangely enough, the walls collapsed on that seventh day. Perhaps it was from sheer surprise.

Christianity depends on an arsenal of unlikely means—forgiveness applied to injury, kindness returned for insult, life given through Christ's death. Unlikely means, then, come as double blessings, for they not only solve our temporary problems, but they also temporarily disarm our defenses through the element of surprise. In our sudden moment of openness, the Spirit might finally speak of some further outlandish plan—perhaps to fell a tyrant with love, perhaps to give thanks during our pain, even to allow loved ones to make their own mistakes so that they might learn the consequences of choice.

As we explore some unlikely means that God has used to answer the prayers of others, may we see ourselves in the same light as we have seen Mary Mack—as one of God's own originals. And as such, may we fully employ the great gift of the surprises we receive to disarm our most stubborn disbelief.

Meant for Each Other

One gray January day, Lucy Lane stood on the empty floor at Bloomingdale's department store in New York City where the Christmas shop she had managed was being dismantled. As the acres of lights, boutiques, and lavish decorations were being packed away, Lucy thought wearily, *That was fun while it lasted, but it's over. I just don't see a future for myself here. Maybe it's time to go back home to Virginia.*

Lucy had lived in the city for two years. Although she had dated a succession of young men, none of them seemed to want the things she did in life. It almost seemed foolish now, but one morning she had come back to her apartment from her daily jog and had opened her prayer journal and written a list of qualities she wanted in a husband: loving, respectful, caring, honest, moral, reverent, successful yet unassuming, secure, hard-working. Many a morning after that, she had bowed her head over the list. Now, as she stood lost in a warehouse of cardboard boxes in the dismantled Christmas department, she faced the hard cold truth. Meeting such a person was a million-to-one chance in such a huge, impersonal city.

The next day Lucy had to fill in for her boss by giving a presentation to a roomful of seasoned buyers. Afterward Lucy thought, *I had such a case of nerves I never saw a single face in the room.* Later that day Lucy's boss said, "There's a fellow named Ted Corwin up in the office who was impressed with your presentation. He wants to meet you to talk over a job opening out at the Garden City store."

Upstairs in the office, a young man in his thirties with wavy brown hair, wire-rimmed glasses, and a thoroughly pleasant smile introduced himself to Lucy. As their eyes met, a strange thought dropped into Lucy's mind: *He's the one you're going to marry.*

Lucy fell into the chair stunned. She tried to put the ridiculous thought aside, but everything about Ted made her feel so comfortable that by the end of the meeting, when he invited her to come to the Garden City store for a formal interview, she found herself saying yes.

"Do you have any questions?" Ted asked.

Lucy's face flushed, "Just one. What train takes me out to Garden City?"

As Ted began outlining a series of trains and connections, Lucy bit her lip. *I'll never be able to get there. I feel like a lost puppy in Central Park.*

Ted read her tense posture and offered, "Why don't I just skip my car pool on the day you come for the interview and I'll show you?"

Lucy stared back in utter surprise thinking, *Wow, he definitely cares about others.*

Lucy got the job, and as she and Ted worked together, she silently checked things off her prayer list. *He's so patient teaching me to read the inventory printouts. And look how he straightened out that employee who was always late for work without being harsh.* One day Ted mentioned, "A member of my car pool's just been promoted to another store. Where do you live?"

"Sixty-ninth Street between Second and Third."

"Well, how about that? I live on Seventieth between Second and Third. We're practically neighbors."

Lucy nearly laughed. All the time she had been wondering where to find someone like Ted, he had been living just around the block!

Lucy joined the car pool. Her seat was over the hump in the middle of the back, right next to Ted. The two fell into walking together the ten blocks to the car pool pickup in the mornings and the two blocks together from the car pool drop-off in the evening. *Who but God could have taken two strangers with so much in common and cause their lives to intersect and merge until they were spending ten hours a day together?* Lucy marveled.

Yet weeks went by, and not the slightest hint of an invitation for a date materialized from Ted. A fellow employee whispered in Lucy's ear that Ted had been divorced after a brief marriage. "*Her* loss, not *his*," he intoned. Lucy was convinced Ted was the one for her, but she was becoming more confused by the day. Perhaps she was just imagining that there was something between them.

What Lucy did not know was that Ted was trying hard *not* to be the one. Ted's former wife had worked at Bloomingdale's, and when their marriage ended, he questioned if he were ever meant to marry. Since he felt he had failed miserably at making a wise decision in choosing a wife, Ted's naturally cautious personality was on code-red alert. It would take a miracle for Ted to take a chance on Lucy Lane, or on anyone else for that matter.

On February 6, the two had been working together a month when a blizzard shut down the city. Lucy's phone rang. It was Ted. "Look," he said, "the roads are impossible. The Garden City store's closed down for the day. Enjoy a day off."

Lucy knew Ted was interested in photography, so she decided to make the first move. "Why don't we take our cameras over to Central Park and get some pictures while it's still snowing?" she asked, her heart thumping.

Ted hesitated, then replied, "Yeah, that would be great."

The two met on the corner and began trudging through knee-deep paths that had been packed down by other pedestrians. They stopped to marvel at Park Avenue, simply a wide blanket of soft white without a car or a taxi in sight. "Listen," Lucy whispered, "everything's so quiet."

"Amazing," Ted replied, "even the smells are gone, and the air is so fresh."

"I feel like I'm in a movie," Lucy said, "and suddenly they've just stopped the frame."

Against this magical backdrop, Lucy and Ted fell into conversation, often stopping to photograph an ordinary object made extraordinary by the snow—a parking meter suspended in a snowdrift, a small ornamental pear tree turned into cutwork linen. In Central Park, they brushed the snow off the seats on a swing set and went flying into the air as wet flakes melted on their faces. It was a glorious day.

When the photos came back from the developers, Lucy carefully pressed them into an album and wrote "long walk, good conversation, fresh air . . ." *Surely now Ted feels something is happening between us,* she thought. Yet still no invitation for a date came.

The second week in February, Lucy went to visit her brother in Florida. Lucy wrote Ted a postcard, her heart and her prayers saying much more than the chatty words about tennis and sunshine that she penned.

Meanwhile, back in New York, Valentine's Day came. When Ted arrived home from work, he was shocked to find a single orchid in a vase waiting for him with the doorman. The note read, "From a secret admirer. Guess who."

Ted's pulse raced as he carried the orchid to his apartment. *A secret admirer? Who could it be?* His analytical eyes searched the florist's card for clues. He got out the directory and looked up the florist's address. The shop was just a block from Lucy's apartment. *Lucy?* he wondered. He carefully scrutinized each loop and dash of the handwriting. He had been working with Lucy long enough to be familiar with her penmanship. He was nearly sure she had written the card. Later that week when Ted pulled Lucy's postcard out of his letter box, he nodded his head knowingly.

By the time Lucy returned, Ted had calculated his first move. *I'll test the waters with a friendly welcome-back peck on Lucy's cheek when we meet at the corner for the car pool on Monday morning,* he decided. But on Monday morning, just as Ted bent to give Lucy his intended peck on the cheek, Lucy abruptly turned her head and his mouth landed squarely on her lips. They were both absolutely shocked. Neither knew what to say or do, so they climbed into the car as if nothing had happened and went through the entire day of work without mentioning the kiss.

That night as the pair walked the two blocks home from their car pool, Ted worked up his courage and began his carefully rehearsed speech, "I want to thank you for the orchid."

Lucy gave him a puzzled look and asked, "What orchid?"

"The one you sent me on Valentine's Day," Ted replied.

"I don't know what you're talking about," Lucy said.

A dead silence fell between the two. Ted's heart constricted as he looked down the street thinking, *Oh, no! Lucy didn't send me that orchid, I accidentally kissed her like a fool this morning, and now I have exactly one block left to decide whether or not to ask her out.*

When they reached the corner, Ted figured he had already made enough blunders that one more would not matter. "Would you like to go out to dinner on Tuesday or Wednesday? I'm going out of town on Thursday."

Lucy smiled and answered, "Tuesday would be great." Somehow she already knew that things would go so well on Tuesday that they would go out on Wednesday night, too.

Ted and Lucy have been married for twenty-one years now and they have three daughters and a son. Every Valentine's Day when Ted arrives at work, he finds a single orchid in a vase on his desk. He smiles, knowing exactly who sent it—his wife, Lucy. To this day, neither Ted nor Lucy knows who sent that first mysterious Valentine's orchid. Perhaps it will always remain one of life's unsolved mysteries. But there is no mystery that God used the orchid to give a cautious young man the motivation he needed to take a divine chance that would affect the rest of his life.

As we read over Ted and Lucy's experiences, we may have assumed that the prayer work was done that January day when Lucy collapsed into the office chair after that "he's the one" feeling when her eyes first met Ted's. The first meeting was the first answer, but it would take more divine intervention to help the prayers become reality. The same story may be told for all of us.

At times it takes the rattling power of unlikely means to overrule our caution. Unfortunately, some answers to prayer that are right before our eyes are also well outside of our comfort zone. God sometimes uses the power of unlikely means to knock us off balance so that we might reconsider our reluctance. What other means could inspire us to follow the most unlikely of life routes, to jump off the cliff of security in order to take a leap of faith? Maybe God knows that until we take that leap, we will never know the fascinating life that might be ours. Perhaps that is why he sometimes sends us small, mysterious nudges, straight from our Secret Admirer.

Saved by an Owl Attack

John Stokes, of Sevierville, Tennessee, did not need to be prodded to take chances. John had been a daredevil since boyhood, when he watched a TV show about parachutists. He stuffed a sheet into his mother's oversized handbag, secured it to his back by threading the handles under his arms, climbed a tree in the backyard and jumped. Luckily a limb broke his fall. Several years later John jumped off a high hill, this time strapped to a hang glider. Soon he was jumping off the Appalachian Mountains, riding invisible thermals rising from the ground.

John was not afraid to apply the same derring-do to his career. While working as a bird keeper at the Memphis Zoo, John grew attached to a one-winged bald eagle named Osceola, training him to perch on his hand to teach children about wildlife. One day the zoo director informed John, "We only keep specimen animals here. Find another home for Osceola." John found a place for the crippled eagle at a private birds-of-prey rehabilitation center. Then he took a cut in pay and joined the staff.

Once on the new job, it became apparent that the center was underfunded. There was an abundance of only one thing—wounded and captured birds in need of a home. John often found himself sawing another piece of scavenged plywood to throw together a new enclosure to squeeze in a few more owls, hawks, or an eagle. By the third year, John was getting paid sporadically and putting off repairs to his truck. When he did get a paycheck, he would cash it and head for the grocery store to buy some chicken wings to feed the birds and a jar of peanut butter and a jug of milk to feed himself.

One day the director of the center drove up, poked his head out the truck window and asked, "So how are the birds doing, John?"

"Fine," John nodded.

The director drove a few feet down the gravel driveway, yanked his truck into reverse, and threw out, "Oh, by the way. I forgot to tell you. You're president now."

Before John could reply, the director's tires were spitting gravel. He zoomed out of the driveway, leaving John in charge. John says, "I felt like somebody just told me that I could have a car with a blown engine, and I could drive it around all I want if I could get it running."

John was too financially pinched even to put gas into his truck. As he pedaled his bicycle five miles daily along a busy road from his apartment to the rehabilitation center, he developed the same close prayer communion of "Lord, don't let me get killed" that had served him so well while hang gliding.

One morning the only food left in his apartment was some canned peas and beans. As John ate his mushy green breakfast, he figured about the only thing he had left to his name was his sense of humor. When John got to work, he retreated to a tree-lined sinkhole on the back of the property. There he slumped down onto a fallen log and let his head hang over in desperate prayer. "God, you've got to help me. Give me some kind of a sign. If something doesn't happen soon, I'm going to have to close this place up and move in with my mother. I figure I've got enough money to feed the birds until next week."

The next day the telephone rang with hopeful news. A gentleman who had seen a short article about the rehabilitation center in the local newspaper explained, "My mother recently died and left a small amount of money. Your center might be the kind of place she'd have wanted it to go to. My brothers and two sisters will be in town from Texas next week, and I'd like you to show us the place."

The next week John spruced up the center, thinking nervously, "If this money doesn't come through, that's it." Everything went well as the gentleman and his white-haired siblings peered curiously around the compound. Then a wildlife worker unexpectedly drove up and announced, "I'm here to pick up that great horned owl we're taking up to the release tower."

John excused himself from his visitors for a moment and stepped into the enclosure that housed five or six owls. One of the roosting owls was so startled by the bang of the door that it flew straight across the enclosure, accidentally scraping John's forehead with one of his razor sharp talons. Unaware that blood was now flowing profusely from his minor head scratch, John nabbed the great horned owl in the net, handed the bagged bird over to the wildlife worker, and latched the enclosure.

One of the ladies let out a gasp when she saw John's bloody face. John's hand flew to the sticky ooze as he thought, *Oh, no, here I am standing with blood all over me from a little owl. They'll think that I sure don't know what I'm doing.*

After a moment of stunned silence, the gentleman cleared his throat. "Fine theatrics, son," he said.

John replied sheepishly, "No. Really. This is real blood."

The man winked, got out his pen, and wrote out a check for four thousand dollars. And what was the name of the dear woman whose memorial gift rescued John and his birds from starvation? Birdie, of course.

John's story brings up another fascinating aspect of unlikely means: theatrics. Although we enjoy watching theatrics, few of us care actually to live them. Theatrics involve suspense and unsolved questions, growls of hunger in our stomachs, squeaks of uncertainty in our voices, blood on our faces, enterprises about to go belly-up, love about to be lost forever. Theatrics sweep us to the threshold of failure, where we ask dramatically, "How in God's name will I succeed and survive?"

Without the theatrics, perhaps John would have received a temporary cash infusion, but he would not have received a faith infusion. When John prayed, he did not simply ask for support money, he asked for a supporting sign. Was John where God wanted him to be, at this center rehabilitating wild birds? Was God in this work, or was this crisis God's way of telling John to close up shop and go on with some other life calling? In this light, the well-choreographed owl attack might have been unnecessary to encourage the gentleman's generosity. Instead, it may have been sent to answer the life question troubling John's heart.

When we ask for a sign, we are unconsciously asking for a bit of theatrics. The saving check, coming as it did with a gush of blood and a whoosh of feathers, elicited laugh-out-loud praise and the unmistakable certainty that God was connecting with John through one of his winged creatures, encouraging him to hang on and to go on.

Jesus himself often used unlikely means not just to solve practical problems but, more importantly, as a memorable sign of who he is. The story of the coin out of the mouth of the fish sticks in our mind because of the pure unlikeliness (Matt. 17:24–27). When Jesus needed two drachmas to pay his temple tax, he gave Peter some preposterous instructions. "Go to the lake and throw out your line. Take the first fish you catch; open its mouth and you will find a four-drachma coin. Take it and give it to them for my tax and yours" (Matt. 17:27).

The Bible passage ends here, short of the hearty laugh that might have echoed over the lake when Peter reeled in a fish, squeezed open the rubbery mouth, and, lo and behold, there was a four-drachma coin embedded along with the hook! Peter must have had a hard time keeping a straight face when he politely presented the coin—still smelling of fish—into the fastidiously clean hand of a priest. Perhaps after all of the fun of praising God and telling the story in such a marvelous way that it would be preserved in Scripture, Peter prudently fried up the jackpot fish. We can imagine it tasted heavenly.

Today, theatrics are sometimes just what we need. The theatrics of unlikely means put the flutter back into faith, the smile onto our hopes, the amazement into the act of receiving. Who but the God of creation, while answering our needs and wants, would go one step further and gild his own perfect lily with such delightfully unexpected glory?

Clipped to the Front Fence

Laurane Bixby hopped over to her jewelry box in her small bungalow in Minneapolis, Minnesota, and leaned heavily on her crutches. This broken leg had been a setback that had worn Laurane out. Her husband, Charles, had died two years earlier, and she had adjusted to widowhood, managing to get the groceries and get to church, despite the fact that she did not drive and had to walk or take the bus everywhere she needed to go. Then Laurane had slipped on her slick-soled shoes in an alley, on her way to a senior citizen's center, and had broken her leg. Dragging around in a cast that covered her leg from toe to knee, the only prayer she felt like praying was, "Why me, Lord?"

As Laurane dug through her jewelry box getting ready to visit a yard sale down the block, she glimpsed one of her favorite pendants, given to her by Charles years earlier when the children were young. *What a shame I've never found earrings to go with that locket,* she thought.

Charles had been a practical sort, and Laurane could not recall him giving her any other piece of jewelry in their thirty years of marriage. Laurane had been quite surprised when they had been at a post office convention in Pennsylvania and Charles had purchased the faceted heart-shaped bauble hanging on a short chain. The gift shop owner called it aurora borealis because of the stone's iridescence, casting off lovely purple and green flashes, depending on how the light caught it. Laurane had always thought it looked like stars embedded in ice.

Laurane left the pendant in the jewelry box and awkwardly left the house on crutches. As she stood getting her breath at the end of her front sidewalk, her eye was caught by something attached to one of the upright lengths of the wrought-iron fence railing.

What on earth could that be? Laurane thought. She looked more closely and realized, *Why, it's an earring! But why would it be clipped to the railing on my front fence?* She bent down, undid the earring and inspected it. It was heart-shaped and let out a familiar purple and green gleam. *It's an aurora borealis earring like that pendant Charles got me in Pennsylvania all those years ago!*

Laurane glanced down the deserted street. *I guess someone lost it when they walked by. Someone else must have found it out front and thought maybe it was mine and clipped it to my railing so I'd see it.*

Laurane put the earring into her pocket and slowly made her way down the sidewalk, thinking, *Too bad there's only one earring. One is worthless without the other. I guess there's some woman out there thinking 'Why me?' because she's lost one of her lovely earrings and she'll never be able to wear them again.*

Laurane was five houses down the block when she chanced to look down in the grass along the sidewalk. She stopped in her tracks. *It can't be!* she thought as she lowered herself to take a closer look. There lay the mate to the aurora borealis earring that had been clipped to her front rail!

After Laurane returned home from the yard sale, she opened her jewelry box and slowly placed the earrings that some odd quirk of fate had given her that day next to the pendant that Charles had given her twenty years earlier. All three stones were perfectly matched, looking for all the world as if they had been purchased at the same time in the same store.

Laurane threw back her head and laughed at her sudden good fortune and thought with awe, "Why me, Lord?" This time it was no longer a cry of self-pity, but rather an exclamation of wonder and joy that the great God of the universe would do something so unlikely as to clip an earring to Laurane's front railing, to show her that despite everything, he always watches and cares.

In the grand scheme of things, earrings are certainly well down the list of importance. Yet there are times when life wears us out and we begin to think of ourselves in that same, low-down way—small, not worthy of much notice or love, easily lost, not much good all alone without a mate. When our strength, courage, and ability are no match for the challenges we face, we wonder, *why me?* never realizing that even a tired sigh of a prayer can set in motion unlikely answers. At such times, God sometimes has an uncanny way of bringing something right to our own front yard that says without words, *When your strength is no match for your problems, I'm here, ready to lend my own matchless power.* As we hold our newly found gift and wonder in stunned silence *Why us?* he whispers back gently, "Because I love you."

A Cure for the Fear of Flying

J. W. Bray, Jr., from Dalton, Georgia, was grounded for years by a fear of flying. J. W.'s position as the primary sales force for the family slipper-making business required travel to New York and Chicago to solicit orders from major retailers. J. W.'s wife, Emily, kept saying, "That long train trip takes all night. If you want to keep up with the competition these days, you've got to fly."

"Okay," J. W. finally agreed, "I'll give it a try, even though I'm convinced that it's risky and downright unnatural." He made an uneasy truce with flying, but no matter how he tried to occupy his mind on a flight, he never could sit on an airplane without thinking, *What if there's bad weather up ahead?* Then he would start to pray, "Lord, you know my kids Laura Lynn and Jim really need me to return from this trip."

One day on a flight from Chicago, J. W.'s worst nightmares came true. When the plane reached thirty-three thousand feet somewhere over Indiana and the flight attendants were serving lunch, the plane took a nosedive. The flight attendant dropped a lunch tray, grabbed on to a seatback as the plane plummeted and gasped, "What's he doing?"

Fear shot through every part of J. W.'s body. He could hear the blood drumming in his ears over the roar of the engines. *I'll never live to tell this story*, he thought in terror. Finally, the plane leveled off at ten thousand feet, and the pilot's voice came over the intercom, explaining about some sort of pressure malfunction. Although they landed without further incident, J. W. walked stiffly into the terminal with the backache of his life, weakly thanking God for getting him back on the ground.

That flight was J. W.'s last for the next fifteen years. J. W. went about convincing Emily how fabulous the train trips north really were. "The roomettes are cozy, the food's good, and I get to catch up on so much rest and reading on the sleeper."

Despite his praise of the train, J. W. secretly waged an inner battle to cure his fear of flying. *This is wrong. It's unreasonable*, he told himself over and over again. One day he forced himself to make flight reservations. He packed his bag. He drove to the airport. Before he had even parked, he turned right around and drove back home.

Even the kidding and embarrassment from his coworkers about his long drives and train trips were nothing compared to the agony J. W. knew that he would experience up in the air. He read every article he could lay his hands on that told how to overcome the fear of flying. Nothing worked. Things got so bad that even being near an airport made him nervous. When Laura Lynn married, moved a thousand miles away to Texas, and had two sons, J. W. still would not dream of flying, even to see his grandchildren.

During this time, J. W.'s prayers were making just as many U-turns. One day he would ask God to help him overcome the fear of flying, and the next day he would wake up scared that the Lord just might answer his prayer and he would have to board a plane.

J. W. finally accepted the fact that he would never fly again. He had enough stress and worries when his business took a major plunge because of foreign competition. He began eating too much and neglected to exercise. Finally he had a heart attack.

Instead of performing surgery, the cardiologist told J. W. to change his ways by eating right, exercising, and learning how to handle stress. Once he was back home, J. W. prayed for the willpower to change his life. He took up walking and jumping rope. He stopped eating sausages and gravy and began eating fruits, vegetables, and whole grains. He let his son take over daily operations at the slipper plant.

A few months after J. W.'s heart attack, Laura Lynn came home from Texas for a visit. Emily confided in J. W., "We've known that Laura's marriage has always been tumultuous, but it looks like her marriage is finally on the rocks for good."

On Saturday morning, J. W. was in his bedroom in his pajamas when he looked out the window. His heart skipped a beat as he realized, *My gosh, that's the sheriff, and he's turning into our driveway!* J. W. rushed to the front door just as the sheriff asked for Laura Lynn and slapped an official document into her hand. It was a court summons concerning divorce proceedings in Texas. A preliminary custody hearing for her boys, ages eight and four, was scheduled for Wednesday.

J. W. felt like someone had flattened him with a punch. Laura Lynn sank down on the family room sofa and burst into tears. Emily wilted onto the sofa next to her as Laura Lynn cried, "What am I going to do?"

"Let's try to think calmly," Emily said, her own voice cracking. Then Emily proceeded to burst into tears herself.

J. W. felt dizzy. *I've got to go to Texas with Laura Lynn. She needs me. But how am I going to get there? I'm still too weak to drive a thousand miles, and the train trip would be too exhausting. Besides, we've got to get there right away to hire a lawyer.*

J. W. left Emily and Laura in the family room and dashed back to his bedroom, where he grabbed up his Bible. He opened it and his eyes searched for something—anything—that might help him. Suddenly his eyes fell on these words, "Gird up now thy loins like a man" (Job 38:3 KJV). He closed his Bible and opened it the second time and his eyes fell upon these words, "Be strong and fear not: behold your God will come" (Isa. 35:4 KJV).

"Okay," J. W. prayed. "You want me to have courage." A third time he closed the Bible and reopened it. This time he read, "Is any thing too hard for the Lord?" (Gen. 18:14 KJV).

This final passage got J. W. out of the chair and onto his feet. He hurried into the family room and announced, "Get us reservations on the next flight to Dallas." The minute the words left his mouth, J. W. thought, *Boy, that didn't even sound like me saying that.*

Emily and Laura Lynn were so stunned they stopped crying and looked at J. W. "What did you say?" Emily mouthed.

"I said, make us a reservation on the next flight to Dallas."

The household flew into a frenzy as reservations were made and suitcases packed. At the airport gate, Laura Lynn whispered to Emily, "Do you really think he's going to get on that airplane?"

"Sure looks like it," Emily replied.

Emily was right. J. W. did it. He got on the plane, "girded his loins" with his seat belt, and repeated to himself as he flew to Dallas, *Do not fear. Nothing is impossible with God.*

Unfortunately, the divorce proceedings did not go as smoothly as the plane trip. A custody dispute arose. Once

J. W. was back in Georgia again, Laura Lynn telephoned, "Daddy, you'll have to come back to Texas. I need you as a supporting witness."

And so the man who feared flying more than anything else got back on a plane, where he sat reassuring himself about the positives of flying. *You know, the food is pretty good, you meet nice people, and it sure is magnificent to see what clouds look like on top.* When J. W. had landed safely in Texas, he learned that the hearing had been postponed again. J. W. flew home, got another call and flew back a third time before the hearing was finally held.

In the courtroom, J. W. took the stand and gave examples of what a good mother Laura Lynn had been. Laura Lynn was awarded custody. Afterward, one of the jurors came up to J. W. "I want you to know," he told him, "it was your testimony that decided us. I've got grandkids myself."

J. W. mumbled thanks to the man, his heart overflowing with gratitude. *What if I hadn't found the courage to come?* he thought. *Things might have turned out so differently for Laura Lynn and the children.* Ever since that day, J. W. has been flying.

Laura Lynn's divorce crisis was not the only unlikely means that changed J. W.'s life. He explains: "When I was lying in the hospital room all hooked up to monitors after my heart attack, I was thankful just to see Emily's face. I was fifty pounds overweight, and I realized that if I didn't change my ways, I was going to die. That was a pretty good motivator."

J. W. learned that unlikely means do not always surprise us by their improbability, like Mary Mack's instantaneous recovery brought on by a pet poodle; nor by their mysterious nature, like Ted and Lucy's orchid; nor even by their high drama, like John's owl attack. Unlikely means may just as well surprise us by their unpleasantness. Who would view the sheriff knocking on our front door with legal papers

in hand as a fortuitous event that might directly a
long-standing prayer? None of us welcomes such m
especially at the low-oxygen moment we see the family na
on a subpoena and fear is shooting through us like our ow
hot blood. And who would view a heart attack as a way to
a healthier life?

God often has a knack of using unwelcome crises to our
advantage. When we pray for patience, we may be given
more annoying moments in which to practice it. When we
pray for courage, we may be given fearsome circumstances.
When we pray for faith, we may be plunged into a crisis of
belief. When we pray for healing, we may have to perform
radical surgery on our own bad habits.

Crisis turns out to be our answer because it often brings a
moment of final clarity. In a split second, we finally sort out
our priorities. Will we run away or assertively act in faith?
Will we master ourselves or be forever mastered by our own
frailties? Unpleasant means provide the impetus to choose
faith over fear, abundant life over miserly existence, growth
over stagnation, health over weakness. We are far from likely
to pray specifically for unpleasant means, but that small
oversight does not make unpleasant events less likely to be
used by God to our eternal benefit.

The View from Rock Bottom

Unlike J. W., Charlotte Czekala never allowed the smallest
detail to get out of control in her life. Tall, blond, and athletic,
Charlotte was picture-perfect, sitting with her handsome
family in church. This camera-ready world, however, had a
high cost, maintained by Charlotte's micromanagement of
her husband, Bob, and their two sons, Ken and Lane.

At age fourteen, Ken began using drugs. Charlotte con-
fronted him. He promised to quit. A week later, he was using

ged him to counselors, psycholo-
...tritionists. She clipped negative
...ck them on Ken's placemat. She
...where he was going and who he

...ext few years, their family life became a night-
... Ken often stayed out all night, was finally arrested
on a DUI, and had to be bailed out of jail. When Charlotte
imagined that things could not get any worse, Lane began
experimenting with drugs. He was suspended from school
and was admitted to a hospital drug-treatment center. In
the meantime, Ken was arrested on a second DUI. Charlotte and Bob stood helplessly in the jail corridor, looking
at Ken through the bars. "We're not bailing you out this
time," Charlotte said. "Either you're going straight into a
drug-treatment program or you're staying here in jail." Ken
chose treatment.

Charlotte says, "At that point I knew my life was a wreck.
We began attending a support group for parents. It was a
relief to hear that others were going through the same things
we had been through.

"Even though I felt some relief, I felt so powerless. They
told us that our kids were the only ones who could bring
about their own recovery and they'd need God's help to do
it. Even though we had tried our best to change them, we
couldn't. The only people we could change were ourselves,
and we'd need as much help from God to do that as our kids
would need to overcome their addictions."

At the third session, Charlotte mentioned in passing to
the leader, "I allowed Bob to buy season basketball tickets
even though I don't think it's worthwhile."

"What do you mean you allowed Bob to do it?" the leader
asked.

"You know what I mean. I let him."

"I'm getting at your attitude. It's hurting you and your family. The more you control, the more Ken manipulates to keep using drugs. You're always playing God. Do you always know what's best? You've robbed your sons of any practical experience in decision making, and you've put tremendous pressure on yourself. If you want a real challenge, try changing Charlotte."

When Charlotte got home, she walked into her closet to slip off her shoes and broke down crying. In that terrible moment, she realized that it would indeed take a power far greater than herself to break her twenty-year-old habits. As surely as her boys were addicted to drugs, Charlotte was addicted to control. Finally she prayed brokenly, "God, please straighten out our family. Help me to do what you know is best, not what I think is best."

Charlotte began rising an hour early for prayer and meditation. As she watched the sun creep over the pines through the kitchen window, she prayed, "God, you made this day. You control it, not me." She continued going to group meetings, reading her Bible, and praying daily. Charlotte began making slow progress, but not Ken. He was eventually hospitalized a second time. Now legally an adult, the counselors advised Bob and Charlotte to lay down strict house rules when Ken got home. If he began using drugs again, he would have to move out.

One cold December night, Bob and Charlotte sat down and had the discussion they both had been dreading. "Ken's using again," Charlotte said slowly.

Bob nodded, "We know what we have to do. It's tough, but it's the only way."

The next day as a chilly wind seeped through the windowpanes, Charlotte met Ken in the middle of the kitchen, rested her hand gently on his arm, and looked up into his face. "I'm sorry, Ken," she said, "you broke our agreement.

You're using drugs again. You're going to have to find another place to live. You can come back when you've been clean and sober for three months."

Ken went into his room and gathered up a few things into a backpack and left the house. Charlotte prayed and fretted all day, "God, Ken doesn't have a car or a job or any money. It's going to be nineteen degrees tonight. Please let a Christian family take him in."

Charlotte called a counselor, hoping he might say, "Go rescue Ken." Instead he said, "You've done the right thing. God loves him more than you do. God is the only one who can work in Ken's life now."

Charlotte got off the phone and got down on her knees and did the hardest labor of motherhood—the labor of letting go of her son to God, totally, completely, without any strings. "God," she begged, "help me release Ken to you. I love him, but I have to let him go. Whether he gets in trouble or not, whether he gets killed or not, give me a strong enough trust in you to allow him to make his own mistakes. And then let me trust that you'll be able to help me through whatever happens."

Charlotte had reason to be worried. Ken did not end up on the doorstep of a nice Christian family that night as she had prayed. He spent two nights hiding out in a garage attic. Then he bummed a ride over to his drug pusher's apartment and moved in. There, he stayed high day and night. His weight dropped dramatically. His complexion turned sallow. He sold drugs. From all appearances, Charlotte's prayers had gone dramatically and tragically unanswered.

On the fourteenth day, something that defies explanation happened. Ken woke up, came down off his high, and did not reach into his pocket for his drugs. In two weeks of total abandon to drugs, something had been burned out of Ken. He reached for his backpack and left his pusher's house, never to return. This time, he showed up on the right doorstep—that of a family that Charlotte had met in the parents' support group. Through their help and love, Ken made it. Three and a half months later, he came home a changed person. He eventually became a drug counselor, helping others find their way out of addiction.

Charlotte's prayers were answered through the most unlikely of all means. It was easy to think that prayer had gone terribly awry when Charlotte's worst nightmare came true and her son moved in with his drug pusher. Trusting that God could work through such a dreadful turn of events goes against all logic and common sense. How can any good come of our broken hearts as we see loved ones travel to rock bottom right before our prayerful eyes?

God does not engineer falls to rock bottoms. Often we create them ourselves, one willful step at a time, until we are flat on our backs, looking up into the air. It is only there that we may be astonished by the power of the ultimate unlikely means—the rebound of grace and redemption when we finally hit rock bottom.

Rock bottom is well beyond the unpleasant means J. W. faced in his battle with the fear of flying. Rock bottom is scary, painful, deadening. Yet Charlotte's story gives us comfort. As long as there is prayer, there is hope that God can work through even this, the ultimate of the improbable means to answer our prayers.

Of course, all rock bottoms do not involve addicts in the gutter. There are other rock bottoms in life. Charlotte found her life out of control because she was always in control. She experienced her own personal moment of life in the rubble, standing shoeless in her closet. The unlikely way in which she regained control of her life was to relinquish control. In a way, Charlotte burned out the same way Ken did. In God's topsy-turvy way, once Charlotte realized that she was utterly empty, she received a fuller life back.

So it is with God. He often uses emptiness to begin filling, brokenness to begin strengthening, bewilderment to begin teaching. At times we are all prodigals, simply a final collapse away from coming to our senses. Even when we waste away our lives and our opportunities, God does not waste even this. For when he sees us hit rock bottom, he reaches down to the bottom of his heart and throws out his arms saying, "Welcome home, my long lost child!" (Luke 15:11–31).

Living Out Unlikely Means

If ever a man appeared serious about being cured, it was Naaman, the commander of the Syrian army during the time of Elisha. Naaman had been suffering from the incurable disease of leprosy. When his slave girl mentions that the God of Israel heals people, Naaman sets out to buy, at any cost, his health from the faraway king of Israel.

Naaman ends up at the door of the prophet Elisha, where the prophet's servant tells him, "Go wash yourself seven times in the Jordan and your flesh will be restored and you will be cleansed" (2 Kings 5:10). Instead of galloping off to the river, Naaman becomes angry at being given such a nonsensical answer. Naaman's servant calms him down by saying, "My father, if the prophet had told you to do some great thing, would you not have done it? How much more, then, when he tells you, 'Wash and be cleansed!'" (2 Kings 5:13).

The servant's ancient question holds a mirror up to how we receive prayer answers in our own lives today. How often have we looked for some grand answer, all the while rejecting the true one because it is too humble, simple, and improbable? How often have we set out thinking that we would do anything, pay any price to receive an answer, and then find ourselves balking at the gate because the price we are asked to pay is our own humility? The bottom-line question is this: Will we set aside our self-importance and accept God's answer, no matter how outlandish the means? Will we dare to jump in the river even after we have already jumped in a hundred other rivers, or will we turn away in disgusted anger, still suffering from our disease and our pride?

Answers to prayer are here, right before our eyes and quite within our grasp, ready to knock us off balance so that we might develop a new equilibrium of faith. God travels right along with us when we find ourselves on the unlikely routes of life. He is there at the cliff jumping, during the unpleasant moments, and even at the rock bottoms. He has already gone ahead of us, lining the pathway with orchids and jewels that shine like the aurora borealis. As we marvel at the glory of an ordinary object suddenly gilded with heaven's fire, we need wonder no longer if God will use unlikely means to answer our prayers. After all, when we were least likely to succeed in our faith, he chose us to spread the news that he answers prayer.

3

SURPRISED
BY PRESENCE

*"The Lord, the God of heaven . . .
will send his angel before you."*

Genesis 24:7

Over lunch my friend Mary Jane said, "Something
unusual happened with Mother, and I'm not sure
what to make of it. Mother was staying in our
first-floor guest room during her chemotherapy. One night
she got up to use the bathroom, and when she started back
to bed, she collapsed because she was so weak. She crawled
on her hands and knees over to the bed, where she reached
up for the cowbell that we kept on the nightstand for her to
ring if she needed help.

"She rang for a long time, and finally someone Mother assumed to be my husband John came into the room. Without turning on the light, he lifted her into the bed and pulled the covers around her.

"At eight the next morning, John came downstairs and heard the bell ringing. He went into the guest room, where he found Mother tucked in bed. She said, 'John, thank you so much for putting me back in bed last night.'

"John was puzzled. 'I don't know what you're talking about,' he said, 'I slept like a log all night. It sure wasn't me.'

"'Of course it was you,' Mother replied. 'There aren't any other men in the house, and how else would I have gotten back in bed?'

"John again denied having anything to do with it, so Mother questioned me and the children. None of us had gotten up the previous night, either. In fact, not one of us had heard the bell.

"A few days later Mother asked, 'Mary Jane, what do you know about angels?'

"'Well,' I replied, 'I've never thought much about them.'

"'I've done a lot of thinking about the other night. God must have sent an angel to put me in bed,' Mother said.

"Since there wasn't any other explanation, we began to refer affectionately to her night visitor as Jonathan. Another time soon afterward, Mother said that she felt herself falling backward when she stepped out of the shower. She said, 'It was like two hands just caught my shoulders and pushed me back up.'"

The table fell silent when Mary Jane was finished. "This is an unusual story," I said. "But I wonder why God would send an angel to get your mother up off the floor? Wouldn't it have been easier for God to wake you up so you could hear the bell? I wonder why he would use supernatural power on a situation that could have been easily fixed otherwise?"

Mary Jane tilted her head in thought.

After another pause, I speculated, "Do you suppose God had some other purpose in mind in sending Jonathan besides getting your mother back into bed?"

"I hadn't thought that there might be another purpose," Mary Jane said. "But looking back, I wonder if Jonathan was some sort of comforting sign of God's presence. None of us knew how close to death Mother really was. In fact, she seemed to be getting better. Could Jonathan have been God's way of telling all of us that Mother wasn't alone, even when she was unconscious?"

God's Manifest Presence

The strange case of Jonathan Angel brings up a number of startling questions concerning answered prayer. Although Mary Jane's mother was on prayer lists in several states, I would hazard a guess that no one prayed specifically, "Please send an angel to tuck her into bed." On the contrary, everyone—family, friends, and church members—had been praying for healing. It is no wonder, based on the wording of our "please heal her" prayers, that the whole Jonathan Angel affair seemed to come from left field. How on earth could Jonathan be even remotely connected to our prayers?

Presence is easily overlooked as an answer to prayer because it is one of those right-before-your-eyes-all-along gifts so terribly visible that it eventually becomes invisible. After all, we have known about God's presence ever since childhood. As children, we gladly accept what we might term God's underlying presence. Unfortunately, as we grow older, we tend to become so accustomed to the natural order of things that God often uses our own children to startle us out of our complacency.

Such a wake-up call came for us one day when our four-year-old son, Jeff, watched my husband Gordon getting out the lawn mower. "Daddy," Jeff asked, "does God make the grass grow?"

"Of course," Gordon replied.

"Well, Daddy," Jeff pressed, "then why are you cutting it?"

Gordon set down the gas can and looked out over the stand of uneven grass blades. Gordon's adult eyes had been seeing a chore to be done. Young Jeff had seen the footprint of a miracle.

We might liken God's underlying presence to the structural steel of the universe. Of course, structural steel is always covered with all sorts of storefronts and doors and reflective windowpanes. As adults, routine and habit cause temporary amnesia to the fact that there is any sort of divine steel holding things together underneath it all. In some mysterious way that we cannot comprehend, prayer, regardless of the specific request, always loosens the latch, allowing a door or a window to crack open momentarily so that we again see with fresh eyes God's glorious presence. These moments when our hearts strangely vibrate with God's nearness, when supernatural light and peace spread over our souls, we are being visited by moments of manifest presence.

Manifest presence simply means that the God who is already there has allowed himself to become visible again in our critical moment of need. The ways and means need not be as dramatic as an angelic visitation. In fact, God is more often found in small moments when we suddenly see, hear, or feel again.

Presence is perhaps the most prevalent answer because it works regardless of our question. Typically, we pray for cure-alls, even though experience shows that good, deserving people are not always cured. Manifest presence works so universally because it is not a cure-all, but rather a care-all. It is apparent that Jonathan Angel did not visit Mary Jane's household to announce a physical healing for her mother. Instead, he seemed to come to offer assurance of God's nearness through a simple act of lifting a weakened woman back into bed with the strong and tender arms of love.

In His Hands

Geri Gibson of Odessa, Texas, had been praying for a year and a half that her husband Jack would be healed of lung cancer. This particular July day, Geri huddled in a chair in the surgical ward as Jack was wheeled away for laser surgery on a tumor blocking his windpipe. The doctors had warned Geri that this operation was definitely not a cure-all. Their objective was to relieve Jack of the frightful feeling of suffocation so that he might die in peace.

Geri's brother Don, who had flown in from Tennessee to support her, eased his tall frame into the seat next to Geri. She grabbed onto his large, rough hands with white-knuckled intensity as they prayed. Jack was Geri's earthly security, her husband, friend, lover, and counselor. They had been married for thirty-nine years and had reared three children together. She had always relied on his engineer's eye, right down to *when* to lay aside her brushes and sign each of her latest impressionistic paintings. When Jack became ill, Geri told her children that whether God healed Jack here on earth or by taking him to heaven, it would not shake her faith. Yet huddled in the surgical waiting room, Geri felt as if she were the one suffocating. She honestly poured her heart out in prayer, "Please, please, God, I'm begging you to heal Jack. I don't want to live without him."

Suddenly a startling image came into Geri's mind. She saw a large hand extended with the palm upward, much as you hold your hand to cup water. In the hand was a tiny figure. *That's Jack*, Geri realized, *and he's totally well!*

Geri squeezed her brother's hands and said, "The Lord has shown me that Jack's in his hands. Everything will be okay." Don gave Geri a puzzled look as she described the riveting image she had just seen. The suffocating feeling lifted, and peace filled Geri's chest. *Maybe God has finally answered my prayers and is about to heal Jack*, she thought.

Jack was not healed. He died in February. The strange vision now hung in Geri's mind like a cruel illusion. Geri walked around in a mental fog, unable to make even simple decisions. *Jack, what should I buy at the grocery store?* she thought. *Jack, what should I wear today?* Each time she was answered by utter silence.

One night as Geri stepped into the shower, horrible wailing sounds began coming out of her throat. Geri's grown daughter Victoria banged on the shower door in alarm, "Mom, what's wrong?"

"I need to talk to Dad," Geri managed.

"Will I do?" Victoria asked.

"No," Geri gasped. "I'm sorry, honey. You won't. I need to talk to Dad."

Don persuaded Geri to fly to Tennessee for a visit, but as she walked down the airway, she felt like running the other direction. Yet she knew she could not outrun her unsettled feeling. When she was home, she wanted to be somewhere else. When she was away, she wanted to be home. She found her seat at the bulkhead and numbly buckled her seat belt. The seats on both her left and right were empty, just like her life. She closed her eyes and felt again the agonizing feeling she had experienced in the shower the night before. "I feel so lost, God. I don't know what to do. I need to talk to Jack so badly."

As the plane gained altitude, Geri felt the clamp of inertia against her chest. The noise of the jet engines pounded inside her head *alone, alone*. Then a tingling sensation began to move through her left hand as it lay on the armrest. Instead of growing cold, her hand began to warm and she felt gentle pressure as if someone had slipped into the empty seat and had clasped her hand. Suddenly, Geri felt that Jack was sitting right there beside her. Words out of nowhere filled her ear—Jack's words. "Don't feel guilty about making decisions without me. I'm okay. Just do what you think the Lord wants you to do."

Geri whispered, "Thank You, Lord," as tears streamed down her face.

In the days and weeks that followed, Geri's mental fog began to slowly lift. In April, Victoria said, "Mom, why don't you paint something?"

"I can't," Geri stammered. "I can't look at the brushes without thinking about Dad. Painting is too tied up with memories of him. He would analyze my paintings and tell me where I needed to change something. Then he would smile and say, 'Now sign it before you mess it up!'"

One morning soon afterward, Geri wandered through the echoing house and stepped onto the back patio. She was startled to see that the rosebushes she had planted for Jack the year before he died had burst into first bloom. *Jack's favorite flower,* she thought as she stared at the Texas sunshine igniting the colors—yellow, pink, red. Geri stood hypnotized, absorbing the colors, wanting to gather them and carry them back into the dark, empty house. An unexpected prayer rose in her mind. "Lord, if you'll help me find a picture to copy in one of my art books, I'll try to paint."

Trembling, Geri went into her studio and took out an art book. She leafed through the pages and then stopped. As she stared at a picture of a girl delicately dipping a bare foot into the water, she thought, *It's captivating. But can I do it?*

Geri forced herself to get the canvas, the paints, the easel. Then she began mixing a palette. Aqua. Teal. Apricot. Geri touched her brush to the canvas. She applied another brushstroke, then another. As her arm fell into the familiar rhythm, the tension seemed to loosen in her shoulders, and an unearthly tranquillity came over her. *This is so strange*, she thought. *It's like God's power is moving through my arm.*

After four hours, Geri stepped back to view the painting. She was astonished to see a nearly finished painting of the best quality work she had ever done.

"Thank you, Lord," Geri whispered. "Now I see there's something angelic about this picture that drew me. It reminds me of the Bible story about the angel who troubled the waters in the pool of Bethesda so that people could get healed (John 5:2–4). Your hand was guiding mine. I couldn't have done this without your help."

With the astonishing painting as her entry point back into life, Geri went on. Several years after Jack's death, Geri met a wonderful man named Lonnie Anthony. The two were married. Then, four years after their wedding, Geri was suddenly taken ill. Her doctor was visibly upset when he told her, "You have an incurable malignancy called multiple myeloma. It causes tumors in the blood plasma of the bone marrow."

Geri underwent very critical surgery and afterward was in horrible pain. She awoke during the night, her whole body soaked with perspiration. Then, in the darkness, the unusual vision that she had seen years earlier while Jack was undergoing surgery suddenly returned. As before, she saw the outstretched hand reaching down from the sky toward the earth. But this time, the person Geri saw resting in the hand was herself.

Peace spread through Geri's body and she said, "Okay, Lord. I'm in your hand. I think you're telling me that you want me to share this vision. If you give me the strength, I'll put this vision on canvas."

After her release from the hospital, Geri began chemotherapy. As she battled the nausea and headaches, she lined up her brushes and paints. Geri photographed Don's hands—the big, sturdy hands she had held in prayer during the first vision—and clipped the photos to her easel as a model. Then she began painting in a background, an idyllic lake surrounded by trees, set against a mountain range. An aura of golden light surrounded the outstretched hand, casting gold on the trees, the water, and the sky.

Geri was unable to sit for long periods, so the actual physical work of painting was supplemented by mental work. While she rested, she asked God to show her the right colors to use. When she had the strength to sit up, Geri searched the Bible for verses about God's hand. She copied the verses and repeated them over until she knew them by heart. Often she reread Isaiah 41:10, "So do not fear, for I am with you; do not be dismayed, for I am your God. I will strengthen you and help you; I will uphold you with my righteous right hand."

As she painted, supernatural peace surrounded her. She felt tranquil and calm as she lost herself in thoughts of God and how great he is. Finally, the painting was finished.

Geri hung the painting in her hallway, not knowing that the vision had one more mission to accomplish. While she was still undergoing chemotherapy, Lonnie suffered a heart attack. As Geri sat in the hospital waiting room while Lonnie underwent triple bypass surgery, she prayed, "Lord, you know I really need him, but he's in your hands." Memorized verses about God's hands flooded her, and Geri marveled at her calmness. She realized that the desperation and panic she had felt with Jack were gone. God was near, no longer a fleeting vision but a bedrock reality in her life.

I met Lonnie and Geri on a Canadian cruise. There they sat at the next table in the dining room, glowing with health and happiness. Geri invited me to her cabin, opened her suitcase, and gave me a notecard with her painting of the vision on it. As I studied the print, I noticed that the painting differed from the way she had described her vision in one important detail. The hand in her painting was not holding a figure, but was empty, leaving the viewers to imagine that God was reaching down to cradle us when we most need to climb in to be lifted and held.

I clutched Geri's card, surprised that her story had not been about the miraculous disappearance of problems, but rather about the miraculous disappearance of fear, dread, and loneliness. Because Geri had been praying for Jack's healing, she had hoped the vision meant that Jack would be healed and remain with them. During her bereavement, Geri went through bleak, lost moments of utter pain, until the moment God had once again stepped through the fabric of the universe—to manifest his nearness to her through the supernatural clasp of an unseen hand against hers as the plane headed skyward.

Just as lovely was that fragile moment of first-blooming roses and Texas sunshine, ordinary pieces of creation turned extraordinary by Geri's awakened attention to the Creator behind them. That commonplace sight of new roses cracked open a door in Geri's soul, allowing her to consider momentarily the possibility of capturing sunlit colors on canvas. Geri pushed open the door by acting. She forced herself to do the one thing she felt she could not do. She once again picked up her neglected paintbrushes and dipped them into the paint. It was a small, normal act, but in it lived and breathed the God who had been there all along, waiting patiently to again move through Geri's newly liberated arm.

Yet Geri's most enduring gift of presence came neither through the blinding visions nor through unexpected moments of golden nearness, but rather through deliberate and diligent practice. As Geri methodically memorized Scripture and meditated on God's character, she was building a personal storehouse that she could open wide in times of deepest need. In a roundabout way, Geri became her own best answer to prayer. She had filled her heart and mind with promises and reminders of God's abiding presence.

Geri finished her story by telling me, "One day a man from church stopped me and said, 'Do you have any idea what an inspiration you've been to me?' I smiled and said, 'The Lord has left me here as a testimony that he still does miracles.'"

As I thanked Geri for the notecard, I realized that it was fitting that her story end with Geri herself, who had once felt so helplessly alone and who had now become, in turn, that open doorway through which we gratefully glimpse God's presence here on earth.

The Leading Lamb and the Protecting Angel

Mary Mack Brown, whose paralyzed arm was cured by the pet poodle in chapter 2, startled the city of Charleston one July day, when a newspaper article proclaimed: "Woman Overpowers Intruder. Man leaves woman, 82, unharmed." How on earth had this disabled ninety-pounder chased off a one-hundred-and-eighty-pound attacker who broke in as she lay helplessly in her own bed just before dawn one Sunday morning?

From the sagging porch, I could see why the intruder had targeted Mary Mack. She lived all alone in a house that stands by itself between two church parking lots. It was hard not to notice the safety concerns—no nearby neighbors, the broken window stuffed with cardboard, the lack of a wheelchair ramp to allow her to get down to the street without assistance.

Mary Mack invited me into her cluttered living room just as a small rain shower began making a pleasant clatter on the tin roof. As the clock tower in a nearby church chimed half past the hour, a smile came on Mary Mack's face, and she began to educate me on the things that I had not noticed that made her house one of the safest places in Charleston.

She explained how the neighboring homes had been demolished to make way for the church parking lots. "Those parking lot people came by, trying to get me to sell, and I told them they wouldn't have to pay me a penny if they could find me another house with all of these rooms and a church right behind me, and a church right beside me, and a church across the street. God lives in those churches, and he's all around me. They just shook their heads and didn't come around anymore."

Mary Mack went on to tell how her courage to believe that God was always with her had been born way back in the 1940s, on the wings of a song from the open windows of the Emmanuel AME Church, just behind her house.

"There were fourteen of us living here, and I was the only working person in the house. I taught school all week. On Saturday I'd walk up to the supermarket and carry home two arms full of groceries. My grandmama raised me, and after Granddaddy died I took care of Grandmama in a room on the second floor of this house. For twenty years we cooked, slept, and ate all in that one room. I knew I had to find someone to trust in to take care of me, because I had my grandmama to take care of.

"Before they got air conditioning at the Emmanuel AME Church, we would sit up there with our window open and hear the singing on Sundays coming from their big open windows. I don't care what Grandmama was doing, when the choir started singing 'Sweet Hour of Prayer,' she'd stop and sing out along with the church people next door. I knew all of the verses to that song. I said, 'That's what's carried Grandmama through, and that's what's going to carry me through, too.'"

A ticking clock filled the silence as Mary Mack paused to fight emotion and then launched into impassioned prayer, "God, I can't see you, I can't feel you, but something within me knows you're right here." After another pause she was again talking to me, "That song stays with me day and night. Through it all, somebody's been watching over me."

I asked her about the recent night when the would-be rapist had broken in. "Were you praying when you woke up and saw a man in your bedroom?"

"No-o," Mary Mack answered, drawing out the *o* long and high, "I was sound asleep, and I didn't hear the window break in the front bedroom. I just opened my eyes and I could see him in the dark going through my dresser drawers. No, I didn't even have time to pray. But every night before I go to bed, I always pray, asking God to watch over the whole house, all of the windows and doors, and to watch over me. And the first thing I wake up in the mornings, I say, 'I don't know what this day holds, but I know you hold the day. Go before me as a leading lamb and behind me as a protecting angel.'

"The next thing I knew, that fellow was on top of me in my bed. But I didn't panic. I patted his head, just like that," Mary said, cupping her hands as you would pat a small child. "And then I said, 'Young man, you wouldn't do this to your grandmother, and you wouldn't be in my house if you were in your right mind.' He jumped up and sat down on the edge of the bed with his head hanging down.

"He said, 'I'm so sorry. I came in the wrong house.' 'No,' I said, 'you came in the right house. I got a message for you to trust God and don't go around doing the things you're doing.' Then he said he was hungry, and I said go out to the Frigidaire to find something to eat."

"Did you try to get onto your wheelchair to get away?" I asked.

"No-o," Mary Mack replied. "You know, if I tried, he would have had me. I was just sitting here in bed, and I wasn't afraid. I don't know why. I always believe that God is right here sitting in this room, as sure as I'm talking to you. I'm just as crazy as can be because I believe that he will take care of me."

The intruder eventually left Mary Mack's empty-handed after she had offered to give him anything he saw in the house he wanted. Before he left, he even lifted her into her wheelchair so she could unlock the front door for him.

Despite appearances to the contrary, the hapless intruder had discovered that Mary Mack was far from alone. God's nearness had little to do with the stucco walls of churches all around and everything to do with the living conduit in the form of an eighty-two-year-old woman in a motorized wheelchair. God was undeniably present because she affirmed he was there. Every morning and evening she prayed God would be there, and all of the time in-between she acted on it with absolute certainty. Her assurance had been powerful enough to rattle the would-be rapist, her calm pats on his head stunning him as effectively as well-placed blows.

Before I left Charleston, I opened my umbrella and ventured out back of Mary Mack's to see the lovely stained glass window on the Emmanuel AME Church. As I stood over the cornerstone that said 1891, I thought about a group of believers, gathered on the sandy black soil adjoining Mary's yard long before she was ever born, led to name the place Emmanuel. Years later, as Mary Mack and her grandmother sat in their small upstairs room, gathering comfort from the hymns ringing from the church's open windows, perhaps it never struck them as it suddenly struck me that day that the name Emmanuel is one of the most powerful names on earth—"God with us" (Matt. 1:23).

Later, as I drove home thinking about Mary Mack's remarkable trust that God was always near, the rain along the interstate turned into a deafening downpour. The minivan shuddered as a truck flung a solid sheet of water onto the windshield. I leaned forward, straining to see the faint red taillights of the car in front of me, my hands aching on the steering wheel. Then, out of nowhere, her prayer was there. *Lord, go before me like a leading lamb and behind me like a protecting angel.*

As those simple words wound through my mind, my hands loosened. In the middle of that downpour I began to experience what Mary Mack meant when she said, "I'm just as crazy as can be because I believe that he will take care of me." It indeed felt a bit crazy, but in a wonderfully freeing way, to let her prayer tuck me into a snug envelope of God's presence. I began to stare into the blinding rain, imagining myself in the middle of a procession, with a leading lamb in front of me and a protecting angel behind me.

To this day, whenever I find myself alone and afraid, I mentally repeat Mary Mack's leading-lamb prayer, thankful for having met her. For she never waited for some odd little miracle to usher her into God's presence. Instead, she used an odd little repetition she had made up about leading lambs that stayed in her mind until it felt just so, until it seemed she could reach out and pat God's lamb just as she patted that intruder.

We are trained to clearly see the dangers all around us. But have we trained ourselves just as thoroughly to imagine God with us every moment? In the Bible, Elisha's servant was shaking in his boots at the terrible sight of a foreign army surrounding them, intent on capturing Elisha. The prophet assured his servant, "Those who are with us are more than those who are with them." Then Elisha prayed that the servant's eyes would be opened, "And he looked and saw the hills full of horses and chariots of fire all around Elisha" (2 Kings 6:15–17).

If we left off reading at this stunning passage, we might assume that fiery heavenly host defeated the approaching enemy. On the contrary. The army was defeated by just one man: Elisha. Elisha prayed that the attackers would be blinded, then he convinced them that they were not in the right city. He persuaded them to follow him, and he led them right into the hands of the king of Israel.

The army was defeated by God's supernatural presence, but not through a legion of angels. The army was defeated by a single man who simply believed that his God was larger than their army. Their blindness had little to do with their eyes and everything to do with their perception. Perhaps they did not recognize Elisha as their prey because he did not act like a terrified, doomed prophet outnumbered by a horde of chariots. There Elisha stood, exuding enough confidence that his attackers became docile followers.

As we leave Mary Mack's, worrying over empty parking lots and broken windows, a small prayer about lambs pops into our minds. We suddenly stop seeing and start perceiving. Instead of parking lots, we see hallowed ground full of God's presence. Instead of broken windows, we see unbroken promises of moment-by-moment nearness. Finally we realize where the lamb is leading. He is leading us to believe that we are never alone. And then we understand the danger that the angel behind us must ward off. For the angel is there to protect us from forgetting that God is always there.

The Watercolor Moment

We were all puzzled when Judy Guilfoil, a faithful member of our neighborhood Bible study group, was absent from our meeting. We missed Judy because of the wonderful way she focuses her clear blue eyes on our faces and enraptures us with some small slice of her life, turning a family dinner-table squabble with her three daughters into a profound lesson on God's love and forgiveness. Perhaps that is why we were all shocked when someone said that Judy was missing because she was going through a time of spiritual dryness.

The next Bible study rolled around, and Judy was absent again. A neighbor told how Judy had cut down on activities to spend time alone. She prayed. She cried. Yet nothing she did could manufacture that joy she wanted to feel in her relationship with her husband and children, and with God.

The fourth week, Judy showed up at Bible study again, her blue eyes as luminous as ever, her face shining over the simple story of what had happened.

"Last week I decided to go on a picnic with Nancy. At first we sat and talked about our problems and the awful spirit of heaviness we were both feeling. Then I said, 'Let's pray together and ask God for a sign of his presence that we can both cling to.' We joined hands and began repeating, 'Jesus, Jesus.'

"A slight breeze was blowing from right to left, and as it passed, I had an unusual sensation. The only way I can describe the feeling is like a watercolor wash, where the color starts out nonexistent, then builds in intensity and then fades back out. You can't define the exact moment it's color, nor can you define the stages. You just understand that color is there. To me it felt like Jesus was moving his Spirit right through me, and I felt that joyful, peaceful presence.

"Nancy had been holding my hand the whole time and she asked, 'What happened? Where did you go?' and I tried to describe it to her the best I could."

Amidst all of the stunning stories of how God manifests his presence, Judy helps remind us of the beauty of the fragile moments of presence, those moments when a dewdrop dangles on the rose petal, waiting for that small window of time when our eyes might glimpse it fall. We missed Judy so much in our group because she was our keeper of fragile moments, able to explain the small breeze in such a way that we could all think, "Yes, I've felt God move gently and imperceptibly into me and through me, and sometimes I can't explain when it started nor when it ended. But now that I've heard Judy, I know that it was real and God was there."

Judy concluded by saying, "I know now that in seeking peace and joy, I was seeking the wrong thing. Instead, I will seek the presence of Jesus and the Holy Spirit, for that is what brings the peace and joy." We all nodded our heads, seeing ourselves once again. For a month Judy had been praying for peace and joy. Then, in one caress of a gentle breeze, she was instead sent God's presence. In that watercolor moment, the lesson washed over our still, calmed hearts. *Don't pray for peace and joy. Pray for and seek presence, and the peace and joy will follow.*

Matchsticks against Wolves

Alex Gross was taught about God's mysterious presence in the synagogue in his small Czechoslovakian village before World War II, where his life was surrounded by God's constant nearness. Alex could smell presence in the aroma of his mother's chicken soup that simmered until noon on the old coal stove and was lavished out into steaming bowls in the small family tailor shop that served as their home. He could hear presence in the thumping rhythm of his father's and brothers' feet against the sewing machine paddles. And at the end of the day, Alex felt presence when he nestled down under the covers with one of his five older brothers on the bed under the tall cutting table.

Then when Alex was twelve, the village was annexed by Hungary. The Nazi swastika and the evils of fascism appeared in the sleepy crossroads. Most of the village boys were en-

listed in the Hitler Youth for paramilitary training. Jewish
boys like Alex were labeled "undesirable" and were forced
to dig ditches and clean latrines.

One rainy day as Alex and one of his brothers left Hebrew
school, a gang of ten boys jumped on them. As the boys spat
vicious names, Alex was so stunned that he barely thought to
defend himself. The boys finished their cruel sport by throwing Alex and his older brother into a muddy ditch along the
unpaved village road. As Alex felt his face grinding against
the rocks in the mud, his lungs ached in disbelief. *These are
my lifelong friends! We used to love each other like brothers.
Why are they doing this to me?*

That night when Alex's mother tucked him into bed, she
said slowly, "I'm so thankful that you weren't hurt today. I
pray for you, and that's why God's angels are always watching over you."

Alex closed his eyes and drifted off to sleep, trying with
all of his heart to imagine angels in muddy ditches. When
Alex was again taunted and attacked two weeks later and
managed to outrun the boys, his mother tucked the covers
around his chin and said, "Those boys chasing you were
sixteen and you're only thirteen, and yet you outran them.
God gave you good legs. See what I mean? Angels watch
over you. God is going to help." Again Alex closed his eyes,
allowing her talk of God's nearness to counteract the hatred
beginning to tear apart their lives.

Day after day Alex was harassed and attacked by his former friends, and night after night, his mother's gentle voice
painted angel wings onto ordinary things, like the rock that
missed hitting Alex or the rake he had been using in the field
that he had grabbed to defend himself.

By the time Alex was fourteen, the attacks were far from
child's play. When Alex could not outrun his tormentors, he
fought back. One day a gang of boys chased Alex to a nar-

row bridge, where he turned and warded off his attackers with a pitchfork. When the wounded boys ran off cursing oaths of vengeance, Alex threw down the pitchfork and ran to the forest to hide. Later his brother found him in his hiding place and whispered, "Alex, those boys won't soon forget the humiliation of the beating they got today. Mother says you must go away until tempers cool. She says to go to our aunt and uncle in the village of Lavik on the other side of Resvigev. They will take care of you."

Still sore and exhausted from the attack, Alex circled through the forest to the road leading out of the village and made it on foot through the neighboring city of Resvigev just as the shadows of the surrounding mountains were growing long on the valley. He realized with dismay that he was still six or seven miles away from the village where his relatives lived, and it would be well after dark before he arrived. Just as he was standing at the roadside, wondering how he could safely cross the mountains alone, he noticed a farm family with an ox-drawn cart coming in his direction.

"Are you going to Lavik?" Alex asked, burying his swollen hands into his pocket.

"Yes," the farmer nodded. "We've been at the open market selling our potatoes today, and we're on our way home. If you're going, you should walk with us. The mountain roads are full of danger at night."

Alex filed in behind the cart, and soon darkness fell heavily along the twisting forest road. As the small caravan rounded a steep turn, Alex noticed something softly gleaming in the darkness about a hundred feet ahead of them. *How strange*, Alex thought. *I don't see a house or a village, but I see tiny round things glowing like small dim lights*. Suddenly fear prickled up Alex's arms. *Those aren't lights, those are eyes. It's a bunch of wolves, ready to attack us!*

Alex's whole body began trembling as a cry rose to his throat. The farmer reached out a large hand and clamped onto Alex's shoulder. The man intoned quietly, "Stay calm. Let's go nice and easy."

Alex fearfully inched his way forward, his feet dragging as he glanced toward the opposite side of the road, planning to run when the wolves attacked. Above the groaning of the cart, he could hear the pattering sounds of the approaching wolves. When the wolves were within striking distance and Alex thought that his heart would beat out of his chest, the farmer exclaimed, "Now!" and the farm family fell into abrupt action. Alex's eyes were stung by an explosion of sudden light. As he blinked, trying to understand what had happened, he smelled sulfur and saw each face of his traveling companions lit by the bright glow of a single match.

Each of them struck a match at the same moment, Alex realized, *and the burst of light stunned the wolves!* As the farm family held the blazing matches out toward the wolves, the wolves fell back in confusion. After a moment of disorganized prancing, the wolves turned and ran off into the forest.

As the last match burned low, Alex glanced nervously behind him toward the edge of the road, opposite the wolves, where he had planned to run to escape. Two feet from the side of the road was a cliff that dropped off several hundred feet. *Even if the wolves hadn't gotten me*, Alex thought dizzily, *I would have fallen off that cliff and been killed.*

Alex and the farm family reached Lavik several hours later, where Alex was welcomed into his uncle's home. After two weeks, Alex missed his family so much that he made his way back to his own village and crept into his home under the cover of darkness. There he told his mother of the wolves on the mountain road. "Those were big wolves, the biggest wolves I've ever seen. If I had been out there by myself, I know they would have ripped me apart. I could hardly believe it when that farm family drove them off with little puny matchsticks."

There was a long pause as Alex's mother let her breath slow. Then she looked up toward the ceiling and smiled, "See. God answers prayer. He had angels watching over you."

When Alex was fifteen, his family was forced to move from their home to a ghetto that was nothing more than an open brick yard. From there they were sent to Auschwitz and later to Buchenwald. Alex was sixteen and a half and slowly starving to death when the Germans abandoned Buchenwald and a group of African-Americans drove a tank into the camp. Growing up in an isolated village, Alex had never before seen a black man. When the uniform of an American soldier appeared out of the tank, Alex thought, *Oh, my! God finally sent Mama's angels. I didn't know angels are black!*

Eventually one of the "angels" lifted Alex, laid him on a cot, put an army blanket over his shivering body, and began spooning food out of a can to his mouth. "They gave us water to drink," Alex said softly. "I hadn't had water in a long time, and to me, it tasted like one of the best sugared drinks in the world. Those GIs were absolutely unbelievable."

Fifty years later as Alex concluded his story with his delicate hands folded on his spotless white kitchen table, it was easy to see the fifteen-year-old boy in his thin, impeccably dressed frame. He explained, "I never grew any bigger than a fifteen-year-old because of starvation in the concentration camp."

One minute Alex was breaking my heart, telling how his parents, grandparents, aunts, and uncles had all been killed. Then he said reverently, "If there ever were an angel, it was my mother. Even faced with hatred that eventually led to her death at Auschwitz, she could always see the wings of angels."

Next, a twinkle stole into his eye, and he told me the chewing gum story. "The first thing the GI did was shove a piece of chewing gum in my mouth. Well, I'd never had chewing gum in my whole life. It tasted so good, I swallowed it!"

As I left Alex's town house and went out to my minivan in the darkness, I felt numb from the enormity of the atrocities he had endured. Then, amidst the haunted darkness, the chewing gum story reappeared in my mind in all of its brilliance. I could picture young Alex lying on the windswept ground, comatose from starvation, abuse, slave labor, disease, and inhumanity. I imagined a GI unfolding his large frame out of a tank. His horrified eyes fall onto the boy who is more dead than alive. In a moment of overflowing compassion, the GI pauses and his hands search his pockets. He feels a thin piece of chewing gum. *Gum?* he thinks. *The kid is starving. What good will gum do?* But the soldier has endured racial hatred himself, so he lets his heart overrule his head. His big capable hands slip the wrapper from the gum as he undoes the foil. A sweet smell of mint lingers on his fingers as his shaking hand pries the gum into the boy's mouth.

In that moment, all time stops. The GI watches the boy's face begin to awaken. He sees the dull eyes brighten. The jaws slowly begin to move. Suddenly, the whole sunken face is moving furiously to chew up the strange, rubbery morsel. Then, all at once, the gum is gone in a ravenous gulp.

A smile springs to the GI's weary face as he realizes that the boy has missed the whole point of chewing gum. But as an answering smile lines the boy's cracked lips, the soldier realizes that the boy has not missed the point at all. For in that moment of sweet exchange, the boy has received not just gum from the GI, but the first act of human kindness since being torn from his parents at the Auschwitz rail depot. Through a single stick of gum, the boy has for a brief moment again felt at home with his mother, village, synagogue, and God.

As the soldier prepares to lift the sixty-pound skeleton of a boy, perhaps he absentmindedly sticks the empty gum wrapper back into his pocket, never realizing that it is no longer paper but suddenly spun of the most wonderful material in the universe. For the paper has been turned into angel wings by his small act of human compassion, spoken into existence long ago by a mother tucking a blanket around her son with stories of angels in the face of a world gone mad.

In our times of deepest darkness, we often question God for sending us ridiculously tiny things like matchsticks and gum sticks to fight giants like wolves and starvation and hatred. We had hoped and prayed for larger, much more intimidating weapons. Yet there we stand, facing the hideous, unpardonable absences of human kindness with a single humble matchstick. Just when we think it is so terribly inadequate, our tiny weapon blazes brightly and bravely against the darkness. At last we learn that this ordinary trifle that God has put into our hands is not really the weapon at all, but rather a channel. Out of it flows the contents of a good human heart, empowered to fearlessly love until the darkness flees in terror from the dazzling presence of the Almighty.

Alive and Present while Dead

Amanda Perry sat conversing with me in her Valdosta, Georgia, home, looking remarkably young and healthy considering her recent death. At first I thought I was investigating a near-death experience, but after listening to Amanda and her mother Becky, I am convinced that Amanda had not been just nearly dead, she had actually been dead for at least fourteen minutes or longer.

Amanda's death happened on Friday, November 11, 1999, in a hospital isolation room full of frantic doctors and nurses trying to reverse a deadly allergic reaction. On Thursday, Becky had driven twenty-eight-year-old Amanda to a doctor's appointment. Because Amanda had developed a life-threatening allergy to latex from repeated exposure through her work as a veterinarian, they rushed in and out of the building to prevent her from inhaling airborne latex particles.

Everything checked out normally at the doctor's visit, but as Becky pulled into a fast food restaurant, Amanda began having an allergic reaction. Amanda says, "I knew immediately I was in trouble. My lungs got so tight, I thought both of them had collapsed. I told Mama, 'Get me to the hospital, quick!'

"The hospital was only five minutes away, but by the time I got there, I was gasping for breath. Mama ran in to tell the staff to get a latex-free isolation room ready. I called my Sunday school teacher on the cell phone and managed to say, 'Just pray!'

"By the time I was in the hospital room, my arms and legs were purple-red, and my hands were so swollen my rings wouldn't come off. They gave me a high dose of medicine. Nothing happened. I had an oxygen mask over my face but I kept saying, 'Do something! I can't breathe.'"

At this point Becky continued the story. "Amanda was incoherent and in respiratory distress all night. She just got worse and worse, and by the next morning I kept asking, 'Amanda, are you still with us?' When the doctor put a tube down her throat, her heart immediately stopped. A nurse yelled 'Code 99!' and the room got wild. They rushed in a cart with a machine to jolt her heart and yelled 'charge' and then 'clear' and Amanda's whole body jumped as the electricity passed through her chest. Ten doctors and nurses were cutting and jabbing because they couldn't find a vein to start an

IV. Finally a doctor just poured the medicine in the tube in Amanda's throat and it came pouring back out of the tube like an erupting volcano.

"Dr. Adcock, who is Amanda's gynecologist, was standing at the foot of the bed, helping a nurse note the time of each procedure. They gave Amanda shock after shock with the paddles, but her heart wouldn't restart. When they gave Amanda the tenth shock as the nurse called out, 'Fifteen minutes,' I feared too much time had passed to bring Amanda back. Then all of a sudden, the line on the heart monitor jumped, and Amanda's heart started beating again on its own."

Becky went on, "Even though her heart was beating, her arms and legs looked so awful from oxygen deprivation that I was worried sick. A pulmonologist came in and looked at Amanda and said, 'Mrs. Perry, I'm very good at what I do, but your daughter won't make it through the night. Even if by some miracle she does survive, there is a real threat of lung damage, possible brain damage, and the loss of her hands and feet.'

"I was calm. I hadn't cried. I stood there and thought what a good girl Amanda had been. By now, family and friends were in the hallway, and they allowed several people into the room. Two dear friends came in and said, 'Let's pray life, not death.'

"Dr. Adcock said, 'I've done everything I can for her medically, but I haven't prayed to the Great Healer yet.' Dr. Adcock leaned over Amanda and started praying in her ear."

Meanwhile, Amanda knew nothing of what was happening in the hospital room because she was not there. "I remember the doctor telling me he was going to put the tube down my throat, and I remember begging him to promise me that he wouldn't put me on a respirator if I wasn't going to recover. As soon as I said that, immediately I was in heaven.

"The closest thing I can compare it to was like when you're flying in a plane and it goes through a cloud and it's solid white and you can't see anything but it's still bright and full of light. I was being approached by a brilliant presence. It wasn't a form so much as it was a glowing light and it was whiter than the surrounding area, much more brilliant and so pure. It seemed it only took a second to approach.

It's Jesus! I thought. But it wasn't like I was just meeting him, it was like he suddenly encapsulated me. I was being cradled by Jesus, and I felt this incredible feeling of peace. I'd never felt anything like it. I can't really describe it. It was just so comforting, and nothing else was real or mattered anymore. My hurting body was gone, and I didn't have to struggle to breathe. I was just there. I was fine, and nothing was wrong. I was in complete peace."

Back in the hospital, Amanda lived through the night, and a steady stream of friends came to support the Perry family in the intensive-care waiting room.

Becky continues, "The doctors decided to take Amanda off the drugs briefly so they could evaluate her condition. At three A.M. on Sunday Amanda opened her eyes. She still had a tube down her throat, so they gave us a card with letters in case she had the ability to spell out a message."

Amanda says, "I never felt any movement or traveling back. I went from being in heaven to being on earth, in a hospital room in the middle of the night, where I found myself all hooked up to tubes and monitors."

After each family member had each spent a tearful moment with Amanda, Becky said, "Amanda, did you know that you died?"

Amanda nodded *yes*.

"Did you see a bright light?" Becky asked.

Amanda nodded *yes* again.

"Did you see Jesus?"

Amanda gave a vigorous nod *yes*.

"Did you know when you came back?"

Amanda shook her head *no*.

Becky was so startled that she went out to the car and got her video camera and taped the same questions and answers, thinking it would be a reassurance to them if Amanda soon died.

Amanda did not go back to heaven. Instead she went home to her own house the following day. Every doctor who attended Amanda said, "There's no medical reason for her to be alive."

Amanda's recovery is truly miraculous, but the most astounding part is what she encountered on the other side of eternity. We often dread that final lonely journey of death, but after hearing how Amanda left the hospital and traveled to a place of brilliant light, we are comforted. It is possible that on that day we will never again be alone, for we will be encapsulated in the actual presence of God. For in the same way we accept Jesus here on earth, he will be there waiting on the other side of death to accept us into heaven (John 3:16, John 14:3).

When Jesus walked the earth, the disciples tried to shoo away mothers who wanted Jesus to touch and bless their children. Jesus told the children to come. Mark records this remarkable detail, "And he took the children in his arms, put his hands on them and blessed them" (Mark 10:16).

We are those children, eagerly waiting for Jesus to touch our foreheads and say words over us about what fine children we are. As we stand in line, waiting for special favor, Jesus reaches down and takes us into his arms, and we suddenly realize that being in his lap is in itself the favor. There we sit, words falling away into irrelevancy. Simply being there in the arms of Jesus is the blessing. For we have taken one small hopeful step toward Jesus on earth and have ended up sitting in the lap of heaven.

Living Out Presence

We often fashion our prayers around the Scripture that says, "Again, I tell you that if two of you on earth agree about anything you ask for, it will be done for you by my Father in heaven" (Matt. 18:19). We choose a partner and then run down a mental list of what "agreeing" means, and does "anything" cover both physical and spiritual things? Then we go about trying to second-guess our prospects of being answered in various ways. We are so busy playing mental ring-around-the-rosy with prayer that we fail to read on to the next verse, where the more marvelous promise awaits. "For where two or three come together in my name, there *am I with them*" (Matt. 18:20, italics added).

Perhaps the greatest miracle of prayer is not asking for and receiving what we want, but rather receiving God. Before the first word is out of our mouth, before the first answer arrives, prayer has already caused the most glorious of all wonders to dawn upon us. For the moment we join hands in prayer, God himself quietly steps into the room, and we are no longer bound by earth or time.

4

SURPRISED
BY A WORD

*The Word became flesh and made
his dwelling among us . . . full of
grace and truth.*

John 1:14

As Margaretta neared the Vail, Colorado, ski slopes, her cheeks burned in embarrassment as she remembered the gift-shop pin that her traveling companions had given her on a previous trip. The pin depicted a chicken with a pair of skis over its wing, running off toward the lodge.

The day Margaretta earned the chicken pin, her companions had persuaded her to take the lift to the top of the intermediate slope. As she dizzily looked down over the steep incline, she thought, *This slope drops off so suddenly there will be nothing but empty space under the tips of my skis.* She screamed to the fellow who had urged her to try the slope, "Why on earth did you drag me up here? There's no way I can ski down this!" She collapsed into the snow on the edge of the run and refused all assistance from her husband or their companions. Finally she wiped her freezing face, staggered to her feet, and started a terrified zig-zag across the slope, never letting her skis point straight downward. Although Margaretta later laughed nervously when her friends presented her the chicken pin, the pin was a fitting symbol of the uncontrollable feelings of fear she often battled.

This return ski trip was more than just an afternoon of recreation; it was Margaretta's chance to do better, her chance to win a small victory. "Lord, help me conquer my fear. Give me your peace," she prayed for the thousandth time as her husband parked the car at the base of the mountain.

Margaretta came by her fears honestly. She could vividly recall the first time fear had gripped her at age seven. That day she saw her five-year-old brother's limp body being pulled out of a swimming pool after being underwater for ten minutes. Margaretta's mother urgently told Margaretta and the other children, "Go over to the steps and pray." Margaretta huddled with the others on the concrete steps, praying the Lord's Prayer over and over again in utter terror, while her mother gave mouth-to-mouth resuscitation to the boy's cold lips. Although her brother miraculously revived and suffered no aftereffects, Margaretta had never forgotten that terrifying moment.

Years later when she became a mother herself, fear washed over her if she glanced out the kitchen window and failed to immediately count all four of her children safely at play in her fenced backyard.

As Margaretta's boots crunched on the snow on the way to the gondola, she continued to pray against panic. She fought apprehension as she secured her skis to the gondola; she tried to make small talk as the gondola jerked across the cable to ascend and swing out into thin air over the treetops. She prayed as sweat formed inside her gloves as she clung tightly to the gondola seat.

About halfway up the mountain, the breath of the skiers began to condense on the gondola glass. Right where Margaretta had been staring uneasily at the treetops and cliffs, a pair of curved lines with a few words within them began to appear on the glass. Apparently an earlier passenger had written a message with his or her finger on the glass, and the oily traces had left an invisible mark on the glass, visible once again only when the windows fogged over. The vanished finger had drawn the shape of a heart. Inside the heart it said: *Jesus loves you.*

Suddenly Margaretta's pounding heart began to slow as she looked at the imposing mountainside through that small damp heart with words of love at the center. Her hand loosened on the seat, and the circulation tingled back into her fingers. Margaretta calmed, convinced that the message on the window was a direct answer to her prayers for help. The great God who could make such a personal message materialize out of thin air could surely give her the courage and strength to face her fears. That day Margaretta skied down the mountain with new resolve, her downhill journey mysteriously helped by a few simple words breathed into existence on a steamed-up window.

Words from on High

How could Margaretta's prayer for courage have been answered by three words that owed their existence to humidity and temperature? More to the point, does God answer prayer by speaking personally to us via words we can easily comprehend?

Words themselves are nothing short of miraculous. I had not given much thought to the invisible power of words until the day I helped my third grader, John, study for a science test on matter. At the bottom of the page, we encountered this question: "Name something that is not made up of matter." John copied from the book with careful cursive, "Words, and the ideas and feelings they express."

In that moment, I found myself open to awe over simple words. Every day we carelessly write, speak, read, hear, and ignore thousands of words, never once thinking of them as occupying a stranger, less concrete plane of existence, never once wondering if they might be answers to our prayers. Yet words and our ability to use complex language set us on the highest rung in the animal kingdom. The Bible says words shape reality (Ps. 33:6). Words are also the building blocks of faith (Deut. 30:14). More importantly, in some mysterious way that we can never fully comprehend, Jesus himself is described as the Word (John 1:1).

We view speech as uniquely human and assume that words require vocal chords to form them, schooled hands to write them, or human minds to think them up. Yet there are countless examples in the Bible of God's voice speaking directly to humans, (including Adam in Genesis 3:9, Moses in Exodus 3:4–12 and Saul in Acts 9:4). In one unusual case, God spoke through the mouth of a donkey (Num. 22:28). There are hints that even inanimate objects have the untapped ability to burst forth in praise. During his triumphal entry into Jerusalem, Jesus says, "I tell you if they [the disciples] keep quiet, the stones will cry out" (Luke 19:40; see also Ps. 98:8). Even hand-writing can appear out of nowhere (Dan. 5:5; see also Exod. 32:16). The Bible clearly shows that in the same way we, the creatures, have the ability to empty out our hearts in words and thoughts to the Creator, he, the Almighty, can likewise pour out his thoughts and desires to us through natural and supernatural means.

Once we start looking, divine answers have a way of pop-ping up in any form that a word may take. The heavenly mes-sage may be spoken, written, or it may simply be whispered in our minds so subtly that we imagine we are thinking it up ourselves.

We fully expect to hear helpful words from those near and dear to us, those whose wisdom and faith we have long ad-mired. Yet God has a delightful way of catching us off guard by sometimes sending us an assurance from the lips of a total stranger who knows nothing of our problems and fears.

Such was the case the day I worriedly prayed for safety concerning a long car trip I was to undertake alone the next day in my minivan. The phone on my desk jangled, and a stranger asked, "Is Van Angel there?"

"I'm sorry, you have the wrong number," I answered. The stranger then proceeded to repeat my telephone number. It was only after I had hung up that I thought, with a laugh, *I drive a van. Maybe I'm the one who's mistaken. He definitely dialed my number. God is letting me know that a van angel is here, ready to go with me tomorrow.*

On a more mysterious note, audible words may come when we are utterly alone, leaving us to wonder with a shiver if per-haps the Lord or one of his angels has spoken to us directly.

Although I personally have never heard such an audible answer to prayer, over the years of investigating stories of faith, I have met perhaps half a dozen people who report hearing such a voice.

One of the more intriguing cases happened to Helen Ortega, who was a devoted member of a sect for twenty years before becoming a Christian. Once converted, Helen was eager to know everything there is to know about Christianity. But she remained terribly confused by the idea of the Trinity, having been taught that this cornerstone of Christianity was illogical, diabolical nonsense.

One day Helen went into the bathroom in her Bakersfield, California, home, knelt down, and planted her elbows on the rim of the tub. There she prayed, "God, I've got to know. Is the Trinity real?" After half an hour of earnest prayer, Helen was stunned to hear precisely three words: "We are one." Immediately Helen blabbered back a string of troublesome questions. Again the voice repeated, "We are one." Helen finally got to her feet, having already received a lifetime's worth of teaching in three small words spoken for her ears alone.

Perhaps one of the most unexpected sources of audible words is the one that is not exactly right *before* our eyes but quite literally right *below* our eyes in the form of our own lips. Sometimes the words fall from our own mouths as we unintentionally say exactly what we most need to hear. It happened that way with my father one night during my girlhood as he waited for my teenage sister Susan to return after violating her curfew. As the hands of the clock swept past eleven, Dad became angrier. When Susan finally came through the storm door, my father opened his mouth to deliver a well-deserved scolding and was shocked to hear four unplanned words tumble from his lips that changed the whole atmosphere of what was to follow. "Susan, I love you," he found himself saying.

Written words, too, have a way of catching us unawares anywhere something might be scrawled or printed. We might glimpse a message on a street sign, a headline, a book, or a bumper sticker. Words may jump off a newspaper page or greet us from a message written in the sand. One day when my husband, Gordon, was being considered for a new job, I was looking up a number in the small Athens, Georgia, phone book when my eyes fell on an unusual indexing name on the top of the local phone-book page. There in black and white it said, "Pray, Karen." Startled, I did just that. I closed the phone book and prayed. We were disappointed when Gordon did not get the job but were thankful when he eventually got another that was a better opportunity. Several months later when the new phone books came out, I turned to the *P* section to see if the woman by the name of Karen Pray was still listed. Not only was she no longer an indexing name in bold letters at the top of the page, she was no longer listed at all.

Lastly, a word may be "dropped into our mind," as author Catherine Marshall used to say, when the inner voice of the Holy Spirit speaks specifically to us in the most intimate of settings: in our own thoughts and souls. As an example, one day I was becoming frustrated trying to write my share of the devotionals for a yearly volume. Finally I complained to God in prayer, "I really don't have that much to say." Immediately an answering thought came into my mind, "Yes, but you have plenty to learn." That one thought lead to a productive writing day as I considered my current life questions as a fellow searcher and not as a teacher.

In this chapter, we will explore some of the unique ways God answers prayer through a single word or through a series of words. For the time being, we will not focus on words that come from the Bible, since we will later devote a chapter on how Scripture verses often become direct answers to prayer.

Whatever form the words take—spoken, written, or dropped into our minds—the precepts remain the same: God is responding to our prayers. The prayer lives of the people in this chapter took a quantum leap the day they allowed their hearts to be set on fire by ordinary words, made extraordinary by God's power. Let us look for our word, just as that heart materialized in front of Margaretta's eyes out of nothingness onto the frigid gondola window.

The Words beyond the Golden Doors

One October night in 1981, Jeff Wierenga awoke from a disturbing dream in his Grand Haven, Michigan, home. In the dream, Jeff was standing on the south side of his house as he watched a tornado move across the northern sky. Next, he was walking through a forest that had been devastated by the tornado. As he passed the felled trees, he was puzzled to see that the limbs still had new green leaves growing on them, as if the trees, though broken, still grew and lived.

That's the second time I've had this dream, Jeff thought. *I wonder if it's some sort of message.* Jeff had first dreamed about the tornado back in the spring in his small apartment near the Georgia Tech campus where he was enrolled in graduate studies in architecture. Back then Jeff's life had been normal with the exception of a nasty case of the flu. But soon after the tornado dream, Jeff could barely walk a block without gasping for breath. When he went to the doctor, he was shocked when he was told that the flu virus had attacked his heart, causing a serious, incurable condition called cardiomyopathy.

Jeff followed the doctor's orders and moved back home to Michigan to recover. Here it was October, and the strange dream had repeated itself—the house, the tornado, the broken trees, the puzzling green leaves.

Months slowly passed, and Jeff failed to improve. He prayed to recover, but instead grew weaker. One day in early March 1982, Jeff's mother mentioned as evenly as she could, "The doctors think we should consider a heart transplant."

"A heart transplant?" Jeff echoed in shock. In the early 1980s, heart transplants had been taken off the experimental list, yet in his wildest imagination he could not picture a heart transplant being an answer to his prayers. He was only twenty-five. All he wanted was to go back to school so he could fulfill his lifelong dream of becoming an architect.

A week later, Jeff was admitted to the hospital with congestive heart failure. His body was swollen with excess fluids, yet his throat ached with thirst. His stomach could not tolerate even a graham cracker, and he was unable to eat or drink. He lay in torment in the hospital room, one moment burning hot, the next frightfully cold. Fearing he was on the brink of death, the Sisters of Mercy gathered in the hospital chapel to pray for Jeff.

On Palm Sunday, as a spring snowstorm rattled against the hospital window, Jeff pleaded, "Mom. Close the blinds. I want life. I want spring. Not winter. But I've accepted death. I'm ready to die if the Lord chooses to take me."

Jeff's mother jumped up and busied herself turning the TV dial. She settled on a religious program that was a repeat from the week before. The two stared at the screen as the minister quoted Exodus 20:12 (KJV): "'Honor thy father and thy mother: that thy days may be long upon the land which the LORD thy God giveth thee.' This commandment has a promise. I think Christians should fight to live a long life because it brings glory to God."

Color flooded his mother's face as she snapped off the TV. She pulled her chair close to Jeff's bedside and said, "I don't think it was a mistake this program was repeated again this week. I think those words were meant specifically for you today. Don't give up on your dreams. Fight to live."

Something stirred inside of Jeff, those big dreams to someday design and build. He nodded. He wanted to live.

By Monday, Jeff's heart had grown as large as a football. A heart transplant became a dimmer prospect, especially since Jeff had no medical insurance to pay the astronomical cost.

The doctor said, "I'm afraid your only chance of getting to a transplant center is to go public for money."

"Call the local TV station," Jeff instructed.

On Tuesday, Jeff was propped up in his hospital bed saying into the camera, "I need a miracle. I see a heart transplant as my opportunity to live a long life."

After the TV crew left, Jeff tried not to dwell on the difficulties his doctors had warned about—the possibility of rejection of a new heart, the expense and side effects of the powerful antirejection medicines he would need to take for the rest of his life, the biopsies and heart catheterizations he would have to undergo, the tendency of others to disengage emotionally from heart transplant recipients because they are afraid the recipient might die. *Do I want to go through all of this if I only live another year in really bad shape afterward?* Jeff wondered as he fell into a fitful sleep.

Suddenly a vivid dream began to unfold, beginning with a series of fast flashes like scenes blinking off and on in such rapid-fire succession that they could not be perceived. Jeff felt as if his body were lying on something like a recliner. He looked to one side, and his attention was riveted to hatch-like doors upholstered in golden fabric. The doors began slowly closing from top to bottom, like something Jeff had seen in a spy movie. Fear gripped him. The upholstery reminded Jeff of the interior of a casket. *Is this the end? Am I seeing the jaws of death?* Jeff wondered. In terror, Jeff shook himself awake.

As the ceiling of the hospital came back into dim focus, he fumbled for the call button. For some inexplicable reason, his kidneys had begun to function. Suddenly Jeff found himself hungry. He ordered a dinner tray.

That evening Jeff was sitting up, eating chicken, when his mother came in with the doctor. "Great news!" the doctor said. "You've been accepted at the University of Pittsburgh for a heart transplant. They've accepted you without demanding the money for the operation up front."

"That's fantastic!" Jeff said.

The doctor went on, "The only condition for the operation is that you be well enough to make the flight. This morning I wouldn't have judged you strong enough to go, but this evening for some reason you seem to be coming out of congestive heart failure."

At eleven o'clock that night, Jeff watched himself on the local news, asking for a miracle. *My miracle has already happened,* he thought gratefully. He fell asleep, and deep into the night he began having the same strange dream from earlier in the day. He saw the rapidly flashing scenes, then the golden doors to his side. Instead of being deathly afraid, this time Jeff sensed, *It's important that I finish this dream, no matter how it ends.*

In the dream, the golden doors began to close slowly from top to bottom. Finally they met and sealed shut. The final closure that Jeff had dreaded as the moment of death in the first dream instead flooded him with a warm, peaceful feeling. Then, to Jeff's astonishment, a voice spoke two distinct words, "Trust God."

Jeff awoke and roused his mother who was dozing in the chair at his bedside. "Mom," he said, "I just had the strangest dream. I know the transplant is going to be a success."

By noon the following day, Jeff was being transferred from an ambulance to a crisp white Cessna medevac plane bound for Pittsburgh. Jeff was lifted on a stretcher through a special five-foot hatch. Jeff waved good-bye to his father through the opening as the hatch closed. The doors pulled down from the top and up from the bottom and finally sealed shut. Jeff was startled to see that the interior of the hatch was upholstered in gold fabric, as was the rest of the plane. An odd feeling went through Jeff as he thought, *The doors in my dream! My father was the last person I saw there waving to me when the plane doors closed. In my dream it must have been my heavenly Father literally speaking to me and telling me to trust him. I'm going to have a heart transplant, but all fear has left me and faith is flooding in. The doors in the dream weren't the jaws of death, but the gateway to life!*

During the week and a half Jeff spent awaiting his transplant, his physical condition continued to improve. On Saturday morning, April 17, 1982, a team of surgeons gave Jeff a new physical heart to match the renewed inner heart he had received via two simple words spoken in a dream.

While Jeff was recovering from his transplant, the doctor told him, "Cardiomyopathy is the fastest and most deadly heart disease. It's like a tornado going through your heart."

Suddenly Jeff remembered the twice-repeated dream of the tornado and thought, *Now I understand what those trees that were knocked down but still growing meant. Even though my life will be different now, I will still have life afterward.*

So far, Jeff has enjoyed an astonishing amount of "life afterward"—nineteen years the last time I spoke with him. He returned to Georgia Tech and finished his studies, and today works for an Atlanta architectural firm. He was senior project-architect for the Mall of Georgia and is an award-winning photographer and an avid traveler.

When I asked Jeff how those words beyond the golden doors had affected his life, he said, "At the time of the transplant, Mom told me, 'If this is God's will, the money will be there.' She was right. Over a two-month period, the money was raised to the last cent.

"Today those words help me keep a positive attitude. I always look ahead instead of looking at my problems, whether it's another medical challenge or worry over battles with insurance companies. I just trust God and go back to work, hoping I can inspire others. Sometimes when I'm on my travels, I get a feeling I've somehow been there before, and I wonder if I'm seeing one of those scenes that flashed before me in my dream. Were those flashes a preview of the wonderful moments of new life God was giving me?"

We are definitely inspired by Jeff, riveted to his story by those other-earthly words beyond the golden doors. What Jeff received might be termed enlightening words that came to him as an answer to prayer. The minute enlightening words reach us, something electrical happens. Such messages switch on something inside of us, whether it be new insight, understanding, courage, or hope. Such answers are neon in our soul, illuminating us with God's power (Ps. 119:105).

Enlightening words are unmistakable, instantly powerful. The moment we receive them, they have already done their work to change us. Instead of changing our circumstances, enlightening words change our perspective, widen our vision, diminish our darkness, and warm our souls. Enlightening words are seldom long or complex, but they stay with us long into the night, and just two simple words, *Trust God*, can last an entire lifetime.

Striking Out at the Ball Field

It was a bitter cold March morning on opening day at John's baseball park, and I was soon shivering, even though I had layered on nearly everything in the coat closet. Despite my knitted wool hat tied under the raincoat hood and a pair of warm red gloves, my hands and ears soon turned numb in the damp wind.

When John's game was finally over at noon, I turned to dash for the minivan and bumped into one of my neighbors. She was wearing a light jacket and had no hat, scarf, or gloves. The thought went through my mind, *You should offer her your gloves and hat*. But the instant the thought went through my mind, an inner protest answered, *But I need my hat and gloves for my morning walk tomorrow.* The inner debate continued, *She could drop them off in my mailbox on her way home.* As the handles to the plastic grocery bags holding leftover team drinks dug into my gloved hand, I brushed aside the thought. *If I loan her my gloves, my hands will freeze carrying these bags back to the van. I had to park a quarter of a mile away, for heaven's sake.* And so I smiled a pleasant good-bye to my neighbor and hurried off in my woolly hat and gloves.

I did not give the mental debate another thought until that night when I ran into my neighbor at a party. Our chatter drifted to the morning ball games and she said, "I'm the Team Mom, and since it was picture day, I had to be at the ballpark from eight in the morning until four in the afternoon."

"Oh," I muttered, thinking of the four hours of warmth my hat and gloves might have given her if I had offered them to her when I left at noon.

Then my neighbor said something that made me fully understand the nature of the opportunity I had missed. "I was chilled to the bone," she said. "When I got home, I got in a hot tub of water, and my face and my hands turned red as a beet."

"I should have loaned you my gloves," I said, suddenly knowing in my heart that what had happened that day had not just been about gloves and hats. I had not been simply surprised by prayer; I had been ambushed by prayer.

Of course, I had not known that I was setting myself up for ambush the previous Tuesday, when a woman asked me to help in her struggles to find God's direction for her life. The more details she told me about her situation, the more mixed up I became. Then the woman's reddened eyes had fallen on me for advice. It was not until I was driving home that a single idea had come. At home I telephoned the woman. "I think we both feel overwhelmed trying to hear from God on such important decisions. Maybe it's because we're unsure if we're really hearing from God. Let's both try an experiment this week. Instead of trying to figure out the big message, why don't we practice hearing from God in smaller things?" Then we closed our conversation by praying, "Lord, speak to us this week."

Here it was Saturday, and along the lines of the old Candid Camera warning about somewhere, somehow, when I least expected it, God had answered my prayer by sending me a word. There was plenty that had surprised me about it. Certainly I had not expected God to tell me anything at the ballpark, and I had definitely expected to hear about something more high and holy than hats and gloves.

Yet the unusual setting and the unlikely content paled in comparison to the astonishing outcome. God sent his word and nothing happened, nothing at all. My neighbor was just as cold after the word was sent as she had been before. How could something as important as a word from God have been so easily resisted and ignored?

In addition to enlightening words, God also sends what we might term guiding words as answers to our prayers. In contrast to enlightening words that are instantly powerful, when guiding words are sent to us, there exists the *potential* for something to happen. The astonishing part is that God calls on *us* to roll up our sleeves and finish the outlined work. This, unfortunately, is precisely where things often go haywire and prayer answers fall by the wayside right and left.

When first comprehended, guiding answers are, in effect, merely words. Because words are immaterial, meaning that they do not have a bodily form, we sometimes treat them as immaterial in the second definition of the word, which means not important or pertinent. We discount, question, ignore, forget, put off, and rationalize them away. Thus we can empty guiding-word prayer answers of their power simply by failing to do anything at all (James 1:22).

In the end, there is only one way to know for sure whether the right-before-our-eyes-all-along ideas that come into our minds are directions from God. The only way to find out is to follow inner urgings over matters large and small, even ordinary things like hats and gloves. It is only then that step number two of warmed hands and warmer neighborhoods can fall into place as God waits to answer prayer by waiting for us to answer with our obedience.

Words at the End of the Rainbow

Diane Deans, of Watkinsville, Georgia, sank down at her kitchen table, took out a notecard and forced herself to do something she had absolutely no stomach to do. "Dear Daddy," she wrote. "Just wanted to let you know that I'm thinking of you. . . ."

Tears stung her eyes as she wrote a few breezy lines about how her baby Joni was beginning to sit up and smile. She hastily licked the envelope and hurried out to her rural mailbox, slammed shut the door and turned up the metal flag. As she fled back into her aging Victorian farmhouse, other words tumbled into her mind that she might have more honestly written: *Oh, Daddy, I love you so much, and it's been so horrible for me since Mom died when I was fourteen and you remarried Sarah [name has been changed] and she shut me out of your life. Now that you're dying of cancer and she doesn't want me to see you and you won't even say you want me, I feel like I'm dying myself.*

Diane and her father had always been close. After her mother's death, Diane had seen how lonely her father was when she glimpsed him listening to her parents' favorite record, *Hello, Dolly,* with tears streaming down his face. She had even been glad when her father told her that he was going to remarry.

But Sarah determined to make a new life for herself and Diane's father by minimizing reminders of the old life. Unfortunately, Diane, who favored her mother, never fit into Sarah's fantasy world. It was a relief to all of them when Diane moved away to go to school. After that, Diane found it best not to visit her father in his home. Instead, he would call her while he was at the office, or they would meet for lunch in the middle of the day.

Now that her father was ill and unable to work, however, there was no more neutral ground. Diane had visited her father in the hospital, and privately he had said that he would like her to come and stay with him while he was hospitalized. Unfortunately, when Sarah heard of it, she said, "No, Diane. He doesn't want you here." The two turned toward the hospital bed, and Diane said, "But, Daddy, you said you wanted me to stay, didn't you?" Diane's father just turned his head toward the wall and did not reply. To Diane, his silence felt like a mortal blow.

Diane looked miserably out through the old wavy glass toward the mailbox flag. Only a thin, invisible line of prayer kept her from going back out and ripping the letter to shreds. The prayer line had been drawn on Wednesday night when Diane's husband, Jon, returned a few minutes late from the Wednesday night church service saying, "I had three deacons pray with me about you and your father. I was pretty upset about the way he treated you on our visit when he wouldn't challenge Sarah and wouldn't say he wanted you there. Tonight the deacons gave me some good advice. They said to keep on loving your father. Pray for him. Keep in contact with him, even if all you can do is write a card. Then wait and don't push him."

Diane answered, "But what if he dies and things aren't right between us? I'll never get over it."

"Diane," Jon said, "I know it's hard for us to see this from God's point of view right now because you've buried hurts deep down inside of you for twelve years. I'll keep praying for you, and so will the ministry group at church. You don't have the luxury of time to work through your hurt. You're going to have to keep on relating to your father now, despite the way you feel."

And so Diane began a small, agonizing ritual, forcing herself to write one letter a week, as Jon and the others kept praying. The prayers seemed to have no effect on Diane. If anything, her bitterness grew daily. Often she would find her breath racing as she thought, *What if he dies while I still feel so betrayed? I think I'll go crazy.*

In July, seven months after the ugly hospital scene, Sarah called and said, "If you want to see your father, you'd better come right away."

It was drizzling when Diane left home. After she had driven for about two hours, the sky blackened and lightning split the sky. As the wipers whacked across the windshield, big angry drops battered her truck. She thought, *How fitting. This storm is just like the terrible relationship between me and Daddy. Why am I even bothering to go?*

Diane drove tensely through the blinding deluge for fifteen minutes, each stormy inch making the situation seem more and more hopeless. Finally the rain slackened just on the outskirts of a small town, and the sun peeked through, turning the road into a shiny black ribbon.

It seemed like the sky was split in two—half sun, half rain cloud still showering the truck. Suddenly Diane drew in her breath at the sight of a perfect rainbow directly in front of her, its foot neatly anchored in a clump of pines on one side of the road. The rainbow arched over the road and then dipped down behind a field on the far roadside.

She could not help but marvel at the perfect beauty of the rainbow, thinking, *I've seen bits and pieces of rainbows during my life, but I've never seen a full brilliant one such as this.* At that moment she remembered her own thoughts about how the storm was such a fitting picture of her strained relationship with her father. She thought, *A rainbow is a sign of hope after destruction and hardship* (Gen. 9:12–16). *Maybe this is what Jon meant about seeing God's point of view through my pain. Daddy has his weaknesses. I have mine, too. God, please give me the strength to accept him without retreating or writing him off to protect myself.*

Unfortunately, when Diane arrived at the hospital, her father was already in a deep coma. There was not a glimmer of recognition when Diane and her sister leaned over the bed and spoke to him. Somehow he managed to live through the night. On Wednesday evening, Diane and her sister were sitting at their father's beside when Sarah was momentarily called out of the room.

As the door quietly closed, Diane's father opened his eyes and whispered, "Well, girls, I think it's time we had a talk now."

Diane stared at her sister in amazement as their father beckoned them closer, his face now alert. As they huddled over his bedside, bending near, he went on, "I'm sorry things turned out like they did. I know now that I remarried too soon after your mother died. I thought we'd be one big happy family again, but that just didn't work out. But I've done right by Sarah, and I've been a good husband. It's been a hard twelve years."

Diane did not move a muscle, trying to catch every word as he continued, "They call this thing I have terminal. I guess I do, too. But when you think about heaven, this is just peanuts. I can't wait for the reunion with your mother, and later with you girls and all of our family. I'm so sorry about

107

the past. I love you both very much. Thank you for coming so I could tell you."

Tears began to stream down Diane's cheeks as she realized that over the past seven months it had been Jon's prayers and those simple letters, each an act of will against emotion, that had kept her from giving up on her father for good and never trying to reach out to him again.

"Am I upsetting you?" her father asked.

"No, no," Diane said, "the upsetting times have been in the past. Daddy, I love you."

"I knew you both always did," he said simply. "I love you, too."

They spoke a moment about his last requests, then he sank back on the pillow and closed his eyes. As the door creaked open and Sarah entered the room, Diane's father was again in a deep and unreachable coma.

Diane walked out into the hospital corridor, a feeling of peace flooding her. She thought, *Even though he's dying, I finally have my daddy back.* Diane looked up at the hands on the big black clock in the hallway and noticed it was 7:30, Wednesday night, and she realized that at that very moment, Jon and three deacons were a hundred miles away, their heads bowed in prayer for healing in her relationship with her father.

Diane's story teaches us a profound lesson about the crucial part our own attitude plays in enabling us to receive words as answers to our prayers. Diane wanted with all of her heart to receive a word of love and reconciliation from her father. At the same time, she felt she had to protect herself from further pain. It took the supernatural power of prayer for her to write those short, difficult, weekly notes, and it was precisely those notes that kept Diane in a position to make the final trip to her father's bedside, where she could at last receive those priceless words. The wisdom Jon shared with Diane after praying with the elders could just as well be words directly from God to any of us struggling with a difficult relationship: *Instead of writing them off, write to them. The time is short and opportunities are fleeting. Continue to reach out on your side until they are able to reach back on their side with the words of love and reconciliation for which your heart longs. My word says, "As far as it depends on you, live in peace with everyone"* (Rom. 12:18–21).

Words of forgiveness are the most powerful words in the universe. They set free. They change lives. They change history. Are we willing to change our own history of letting hurt and bitterness stand between us and those who matter? Are we ready to be transformed by prayer to open our mouths and offer healing words of acceptance and reconciliation that others so desperately need to hear?

Help at the Tip of a Pen

Early on Saturday morning, Ted Corwin, whom we met in the story of the mystery orchid in chapter 2, sat in a Memphis motel room under a steady fire of questions from his mentor, George Pickard, who had weathered the ups and downs of the furniture manufacturing business for half a century. Ted had asked George to meet him to talk over an idea of starting up his own company to manufacture upholstered dining-room chairs and glass-top tables. Still as cautious as ever, Ted dreaded the idea of going into business for himself, but it seemed like his last hope. After marrying Lucy, he left his job as buyer at Bloomingdale's and took a position at a major furniture manufacturer. After a hostile corporate takeover, Ted had found himself out of favor as part of the "old team" and had been demoted.

Ted had hoped George would offer him encouragement, but instead he was getting a grilling. Although George was eighty, there was nothing feeble about the hardball questions he was throwing out. "Ted, when are you going to get off this thing about needing a partner?" George fired away.

"You know I have Lucy, little Lucy, and the twins to support," Ted replied. "I really need a partner because I don't fear failure so much with others around me. I hate risk. I'm not cut out to be in business for myself."

"Failure won't kill you. But fear of it will," George replied.

"But what makes you think I can do it? Before the new management came in and I was demoted, I thought handling people was one of my strengths. Now my boss acts like he doesn't have a bit of confidence in me," Ted complained.

George shook his head. "As long as you keep working for someone else, there will always be somebody like him around to undercut your confidence and make you think you're no good."

"Maybe things will get better at the plant," Ted said.

"Ted, you've got the smarts to start your own business, but until you forget about security and get up enough courage to up and quit, we're just wasting our time. No use in me hanging around here until you make up your mind," George said, collecting his briefcase.

Ted watched in disbelief as the motel room door shut. He sank down onto the bed, thinking, *Now what? George has just walked out on me, and it's only eight in the morning. He's right. I can't possibly start a business. I'm stuck, just like I'm stuck here in this motel room until tomorrow because of my nonrefundable plane ticket.*

Ted spent the morning trying to pick apart every detail of his conversation with George. After lunch, he went out to the motel's pool courtyard and sat despondently in a lounge chair, under a hot clear sky rattled by the intermittent thunder of low-flying planes heading for the airport.

Ted and Lucy attended church faithfully, but Ted had always approached faith analytically. You set a good example, you listened from the pew on Sunday mornings, and you used the moral lessons to be as decent a person as you could. Now, sitting there in the lounge chair beside the deserted pool, with his career falling to pieces and his hopes of starting his own business pulverized, he closed his eyes, threw aside all intellectual logic, and started talking to God like he could actually hear every feeling behind his words. "God, I'm forty-two years old, and I've got a wife and children. My self-esteem is gone, and my hope is gone, and I don't have any idea what to do. Why am I here on this earth?"

As Ted later told me what had happened out at the pool, he said, "I prayed and prayed and prayed. I was devastated because I knew to start a business you had to eat it, sleep it, and drink it, and I just wasn't there. All of the criticism at my job had drained my self-confidence. Finally, at about four in the afternoon, I went into my motel room and began to write down what had happened that day."

Ted sat down at the desk and took out a notepad. On the first page Ted wrote down George's questions about his fears and motivations. At the bottom of the page he wrote questions to himself: "How hard do I really want to work? What do I really want in life?" Then he found himself writing a question he had not seriously considered before: "What would God want me to do?"

As he dashed off a few more thoughts on why he felt he needed a partner, he found himself writing a strange and astonishing sentence. "When the going gets tough, my salvation is not internal but has to involve God's help shouldering the burden."

Where did that come from? Ted wondered. The next paragraph contained more self-revelation. "I probably grew the most in my life when I was alone." He went on to list an eight-month trip to Europe, his divorce and separation from

111

his first wife, Lucy's difficult pregnancy with the twins, and his recent business demotion.

The next sentence jumped off the page, as if someone was indeed beginning to speak intimately and directly to him. "Never betray the best that is within you."

By now, Ted realized that his long hours of prayer by the pool were being answered in some bizarre way he had never dreamed possible. *Am I really having a dialogue with God?* he wondered, hardly daring to breathe as he wrote, "Lord, what do you want of me? Let me be obedient. In these terms, 'fear of failure' or security have no bearing. How best to serve? I'm definitely going to have to take some risks, but with God I can do that."

The next few lines flew across the page as if Ted were taking dictation. When he reread the final paragraphs, chills went up his back. His own pen had clearly and unmistakably recorded a call to start his own business, a call that neither Ted nor George nor anyone on earth would have guessed. But the words had flowed from his pen: "Build a Christian organization. Develop that extraordinary respect. Share your faith. Help others grow. Be an example of a house built on a solid foundation. Be warm. Be humble. Care. Go into business."

"Lord, please use me," Ted answered on the notepad.

He wrote down the words that answered in his mind. "I will."

"On my own I can't, but with your help, Lord, I can."

"Do not worry, trust in me."

Ted put down his pen, feeling electricity running through his body. In the course of writing three notebook pages, his whole world had changed, leaving him with an amazing written documentation of God's answer to his prayers. Only an hour earlier, Ted had been at the lowest point in his life. Now he felt hopeful, excited, enabled. Nothing had materially changed about his circumstances, yet everything that mattered had changed in his heart with a few strokes of an ordinary pen.

I met Ted ten years later at the business he had been called to found, Designmaster Furniture. Ted read aloud to me the astonishing three pages of notes he had received in the Memphis motel room. As he handed me a photocopy for my records, he explained, "I have the originals in a fireproof file cabinet."

I stared down at the angular pages of words. It was an ordinary paper and ordinary words. Yet the originals were so dear to Ted that he dared not carry the originals around in case he might misplace them. Ted explained why those pages were so irreplaceable. "Nothing like that had ever happened to me before. When I told Lucy and our parents about it, the only way I could describe it to them was as a religious experience. It was so unusual. It revolutionized everything I had ever thought about God. I knew a little about Jesus, but I did not know Jesus. Today God is allowing me to see things that formerly I was blind to. I have a hunger for the Scriptures. Sermons speak more directly to me. The words of hymns I've sung for years touch me now inside. I am convicted of my sinfulness, and I know that salary is a meaningless measure of a person."

As Ted finished his story, I realized that when God spoke to Ted in that motel room that day, more than a successful business venture was born. Rather, because God spoke and Ted suddenly heard, Ted was reborn. As we grope for guidance to get us through the latest crisis, God often takes us a quantum leap forward by becoming our guide. The moment our ears become unstopped, all heaven breaks out in our lives. Instead of simply meeting our temporary need, God fulfills our forever need by beginning a lifetime of fruitful communication with him. Suddenly a partnership with God is formed, where intimate fellowship leads to daring big things and dreaming impossible dreams.

Ted concluded by saying, "When I'm asked if I started Designmaster, I'm quick to point out that although I was there at the start, God gets the credit and the glory for starting this company. I know myself, and I know that I didn't do it. God did it."

Spoken into Existence

"Lord, I can't do this," Ginny said as her eyes rested on a name on her phone-a-thon fund-raising list of alumni from her college. It was February 1986. "Bud," she repeated to herself, feeling the years melt away as she remembered sitting at the breakfast table while visiting his family home more than thirty years earlier. Years later when she summed up that scene, she told me, "He took me home to meet his parents, and they fed me cold shoulder for breakfast. For some reason, I wasn't the one they would have picked out for Bud. That put the kibosh on the whole thing."

Ginny and Bud had met at college in 1952, when she was a sophomore and he was a freshman. Ginny had been attracted to him immediately, and they had been good friends before dating in her senior year. When Ginny graduated in 1954, Bud took her to meet his parents, and soon after that "cold shoulder" breakfast, their relationship cooled. There had never been any sort of formal breakup. Ginny moved to Mobile to teach, and Bud eventually stopped writing her. As the years went by, Ginny heard that Bud had graduated, married a classmate, and gone to seminary. Later she heard he moved to the West Coast, where he went into business.

Ginny never married but went on with her busy life teaching, furthering her education, singing with an evangelistic group, caring for her aging parents. She lived in Mobile, Battle Creek, Knoxville, Kalamazoo, Indianapolis. Finally she moved back home and took a position at her alma mater. She had not seen Bud since 1954, but strangely enough, she had run into his parents a number of years later when they had come to the college to do some volunteer work. One day in 1981, Ginny had been called to her desk, and there stood Bud's mother. Then she said something that struck Ginny as terribly odd. "I'm so sorry for having interrupted your friendship with Bud."

What was that all about? Ginny wondered. *Why would she seek me out and say such a thing after all of the time that's passed?*

Then in 1985, the alumni director who had been working at the college since Ginny was a student came to her and showed her a change-of-address notice. "I thought you'd be interested in knowing this." It was a letter from Bud's wife, explaining that they now had separate addresses following their divorce.

Ginny's finger trembled as she dialed Bud's number. When he answered the phone, she managed to say cheerfully, "Hello, this is a voice out of your past."

Immediately Bud said, "Hi Ginny."

He remembers me, after all of these years, she thought.

"Are you calling about alumni weekend?" he asked.

"No, about the phone-a-thon," Ginny answered. "But I'd certainly advise you to come for alumni weekend, because it would be fun and lots of your friends are coming back."

"Who's coming?" Bud asked.

"The Harmons, the Greens, the Johnsons, all of your old cronies."

There was a pause, and Bud said slowly, "I'd be too embarrassed to come."

He did not need to elaborate. Back when they were growing up in the fifties, people in small towns in good homes did not divorce. It was that simple.

Ginny tried to encourage him, "A girl we knew came back last year even though her husband had left her. She said it was so healing to come back, because everybody here knew her before all of those problems."

"I'll think about it," Bud said. Then he hung up.

In April, Ginny was surprised when Bud called her back. "Since my mother died last year, I thought my dad would like to come with me to alumni weekend. Would you make the arrangements?"

As the July alumni weekend approached, Ginny prayed, "Lord, you know what my heart's feeling. I'm not sure what I should do when Bud gets here. Please give me the wisdom to do what you want and to say what you want."

Several friends were staying with Ginny that weekend, so she invited Bud and his father to join them for breakfast. When Bud got out of the car, Ginny thought, *I feel like those thirty-five years since we last saw each other never happened.*

Ginny cooked up a hot meal of bacon, eggs, and toast. After breakfast, Bud said to the others, "I hope the rest of you have something to do for the next few hours, because this young lady and I have thirty-five years to catch up on."

As Bud helped Ginny with the dishes, the two chattered pleasantly, then they went into the living room to talk. Bud stretched out on the sofa and told her all about his two grown daughters, and Ginny sat in her chair with her poodle Cuddles and told about the years caring for her elderly parents.

After they had talked for an hour, Bud said, "Ginny, how come you never got married?"

Ginny's heart skipped a beat, and before she knew it, she found words coming out of her mouth, "There was only one person I ever loved in my life, and that was you."

Bud stared at the floor and said nothing. Ginny's heart was beating like mad as she wondered, *Now what happens? I had no idea I was going to say that, and from the looks of him, he never expected it in a million years, either. God, what on earth is going on here? I prayed that you'd help me know how to act, but I never expected this.*

After an awkward pause, Bud managed to say, "Why didn't you ever tell me that back then?"

"It was the fifties," Ginny said. "It wasn't considered proper."

The two let it drop and went back to talking about safer subjects. *It's obvious he's struggling*, Ginny thought. *He seems to have lost his faith.* "What are you reading for inspiration these days?" she asked. "Do you still have all of your notes from Bible class?"

"No," Bud said, "I threw them all away."

Suddenly a thought dropped in Ginny's mind. She got up and took a book off the shelf. "I want you to have my daddy's Bible," she said. "He was a preacher for fifty-five years, and it's not in the best shape because we had it bound and rebound. But it's full of notes all over it, things underlined and things in the margin and all over the front and back pages."

Bud took the Bible, genuinely shocked again. "No, I couldn't take it," he stammered.

"You know the Lord of this book, and you knew my father. Please take it," Ginny insisted.

Bud finally accepted the Bible, and soon it was time to meet the others for the planned alumni activities. During the remainder of the weekend, Ginny and Bud were around each other, but always in a group of ten or so friends. At the end of the weekend, Bud flew back to the West Coast alone, save for the tattered Bible in his suitcase.

Ginny met with a group of four couples and two other single women, and she asked them to pray that Bud would be refreshed in his relationship with God. "He's not happy emotionally, but he doesn't know he's not happy spiritually, either," she told them.

Privately, Ginny's prayers were much more intensely personal. "Lord," she said, "I don't know how to pray about this. I want Bud to be a part of my life. Ever since 1953, there's been something there in my heart for him. But I also want him to be in a relationship with you. If he doesn't have that, he'd just be going from one bad situation to a second one. This is the hardest thing I've ever prayed, but help me be willing to give him up again if that's what it takes for him to find you again."

Ginny began sending funny cards to Bud every week or two, just to remind him that God loved him. When his birthday came in September, Ginny called him long distance. He seemed preoccupied and said very little. They talked for such a short time that the call only cost fifty-two cents. Ginny fought mixed emotions. *Am I setting myself up for a huge disappointment? But then again, what do I have to lose? If God can use me to be that person who proves to him that there truly is a wonderful love that won't give up on him, then it's worth it even if there's no future in it for me.*

The group of ten continued to pray for Ginny, and one day she told them, "If the Lord leads Bud to ask me to marry him, I'd say yes with no second thoughts. He sees the kind of life I'm leading, and if he doesn't want any part of that, he won't ask me."

The following spring, Ginny decided to move to Nashville to pursue her musical interests. She wrote to Bud telling him that she was moving in July. One day in June, her phone rang, and a voice started right in without even identifying himself, "So when is it you're moving to Nashville?"

"Oh, hi, Bud," Ginny answered. "The last of July."

"Well I'm coming east the last of July, and I'm going to make things right with my dad. Call me there when you get settled." Ginny put the phone down, her heart thumping.

Two days after she got to Nashville, Ginny called Bud and was surprised to hear him say, "I want to come and see you."

Ginny had an aunt who lived on the Georgia coast, so she invited Bud to go with her for a visit. Ginny says, "When I walked in the door and my aunt saw that my friend was a man, I could see in her eyes that she was thinking, *My goodness, what's happened to her?* But my aunt is a wonderful lady, and she welcomed Bud in and took us out to nice dinners and told him stories about my dad's family.

"I could tell that Bud was changed. We spent hours on the beach. He seemed relaxed, almost like the young man I used to know, especially when he picked up a big shell on the beach and walked up to a stranger and held it up like a microphone and said, 'Hello, would you mind if I interviewed you today?'

"We talked a lot about his life, about his career and what he wanted to do. He wanted to know all about my work. I just naturally talk about God all of the time, even when I see babies in the grocery store and say to the mother, 'May God bless you as you raise this beautiful child.' I didn't stop talking that way around Bud, and he seemed to take it all in. Finally I asked him, 'Did you ever read Dad's Bible?' He told me, 'I looked through it a couple of times.'

"We had the most wonderful five days together, and at the end he seemed like a person whose whole mental attitude had been revived. Then it was time for me to go back to Nashville and him to Pennsylvania. Ten days later the phone rang. 'I'm at a jeweler's, and I'm only asking one question. What's the size of the third finger on your left hand?' Well, my heart really got twitterlated, as the old-timers used to say.

"The next week Bud called and said, 'I'm coming to Nashville.' I met him at the airport, and we went out to dinner. When we got back to my little apartment, he got down on his knees and said, 'I don't know what kind of love I can offer you, but I would love to be your husband.' I said yes, and we both sat there boohooing. We were married in the steeplechase park in Nashville on his birthday in September 1987, exactly one year after that phone call when he barely spoke to me. Now he's teaching Sunday school and leading a college study group."

Ginny concluded, "Whenever I tell my story to young girls at the college, I tell them, 'Don't put God in a box. Pray about whom you're going to marry. Make it God's choice. Then it's such a joy to just roll over every morning and look at him and to smile and laugh and think, 'What a gift!'"

Through Ginny we, too, say, "What a gift!" that answers to prayer can come to us by our own words. We laugh like Ginny, caught off guard to discover that the words that most need to be born into the world are sometimes the ones that have needed to come from our own mouths for ever so long. We have a way of guarding what we say, feeling one thing and saying another, arguing and complaining about something trivial when there is actually something larger bothering us deep inside. That is why God can surprise us by what comes out of our own mouths when we are praying for his help and guidance.

God knows what is deep in our hearts. Jesus says, "What you have said in the dark will be heard in the daylight, and what you have whispered in the ear in the inner rooms will be proclaimed from the housetops" (Luke 12:3). Of course, God does not prompt us to be brutally honest; he wants us to be faithfully honest. He wants to help us speak words that create love and hope and beauty. These wonderfully intangible things can only exist when spoken into existence, just as God said, "'Let there be light' and there was light" (Gen. 1:3).

I am confident that Ginny was as lovely a bride at age fifty-five as she would have been at age twenty-two. Ginny's beauty is ageless, and the most beautiful thing about her is her voice. I am told that Ginny is an accomplished singer, but I never have heard her sing. Instead, I have seen her hug a woman whose husband has just had surgery and say with a musical voice, "I'm so glad you're here today. May God bless you." In speaking such words, the ideas of gladness and blessing and a sense of belonging to God flow. And as we speak love into existence, we ourselves suddenly can hear it all back again in our own listening ears and hearts.

Living Out Words

If we truly are serious about not missing a single answer to our prayers, we must seriously consider developing our listening skills. Too often our ability to understand God is much like an infant's limited ability to understand his parents. Babies hear sounds well enough, but since they do not yet grasp the meaning of words, they rely on readings of circumstances. If they get fed, they reason that they were heard. If they do not get fed immediately, they assume no one has answered their cries, even though their bottle may be warming. Likewise, our prayer lives will never outgrow infancy if we rely solely on circumstantial answers. We will only grow when we develop the ability to hear answering words from God explaining the reasons behind our circumstances.

In order to receive prayer answers, we must go beyond our assumption that receiving an answer means being sent a solution to our problems. The word *answer* has another quite pertinent meaning. Answer also means a reply. When we only count solutions as answers to prayer, we are settling for a paltry amount of lesser blessings. A solution only works once. A reply keeps on working for a lifetime as we become engaged in an everlasting dialogue with God. The true miracle of prayer happens when we are able to sit here in a fallen and flawed world on this side of eternity, exploring new ideas, exploding old habits, gaining new thoughts at the knee of our Creator.

And so the answering words we receive are not simply short-term solutions but an inner revolution, for we are receiving, like Jeff Wierenga, replies from beyond the golden doors. They may not answer every question in our minds, but they always answer the most pressing matters in our hearts as all else is swept away with one powerful word: Trust.

Just as our dearest friends bless us with words of help and kindness, so God also blesses us by answering our prayers with words from heaven. The words may come in any form, whether spoken by human lips, written somewhere in the world, or spoken in the hidden recesses of our private thoughts. Sometimes the words will illuminate our souls with power, bringing a brilliant instant of hope, joy, faith, and courage into our lives. Other times, the words may be directions whose power is only complete when we ourselves take a chance and follow to the unusual places of obedience they may lead. Words of forgiveness, healing, and reconciliation are ours, not through a sovereign work of God but through a stubborn work of our own will as prayer preserves our sanity during difficult relationships so that healing words might someday flow. And finally, words of love and hope can be the most potent prayer answers in the world as long as we obediently speak them forth to a listening, hurting world.

God says, "As the rain and the snow come down from heaven, and do not return to it without watering the earth and making it bud and flourish, so that it yields seed for the sower and bread for the eater, so is my word that goes out from my mouth: It will not return to me empty but will accomplish what I desire and achieve the purpose for which I sent it" (Isa. 55:10–11).

Today God is speaking a word to us in answer to our prayers. The only question is this: Are we listening?

5

SURPRISED
BY A CALL TO PRAY

"Get up and pray."

Luke 22:46

My passenger in the minivan on that spring day in Augusta, Georgia, was no ordinary passenger, but rather Cathy Barbay, miracle woman. Already in my investigation I had spoken with her surgeon, Dr. Randy Cooper. He pulled a book from his office shelf and showed me that Cathy should never have survived after receiving 314 units of blood and blood products following the birth of her fifth daughter. "A person's liver is nearly always destroyed after twenty units," he explained, his finger resting on the medical journal paragraph

123

that reported 180 units as the official record. "And there's no mention if this person lived or died. Cathy not only lived; she is well today."

As I glanced at my passenger, whose long dark hair and gentle eyes reflected her Mexican-American heritage, I realized that Cathy's life, even before becoming the miracle woman, was a modern Cinderella story. Cathy's childhood had been spent in Texas in near poverty in a single parent home. She was a painfully shy and withdrawn child who usually responded to strangers with a tight-lipped giggle. Constantly needed at home to help with her younger brothers and sisters, two of whom were blind, Cathy eventually dropped out of school in the ninth grade to help her ill mother run the household.

One day the parish priest, who directed a youth singing group as an outreach in Cathy's housing project, was utterly astonished to hear her natural, clear-as-amber alto voice. Without having been taught to read a note of music, Cathy had an enthralling, God-given gift of harmony. Cathy began traveling with the youth choir on weekends, and with each concert as she opened her heart to sing, she made slow, steady gains toward self-confidence.

As a young adult, Cathy moved from Texas to join a Christian community in Georgia called the Alleluia Community. She went on to earn a GED, then finished two years of college before becoming a medical secretary. The Cinderella story seemed to need only the "happily ever after" added when she married a good man named Steve, and they settled down to raise four daughters in a modest home decorated from floor to ceiling with pictures of Mary and baby Jesus in every imaginable style.

So there I was, driving down a busy Augusta street, entrusted with transporting the miracle Cinderella. Cathy instructed me to turn left, and as I braked and turned on my blinker, I found myself looking intently into the rearview mirror, making sure that the car behind me was slowing. Sweat broke out under my hands as I thought, *The last thing I want is to have a wreck and injure the miracle woman. Lord, help me make this turn safely.*

We made a clean turn and arrived at our destination without mishap, and as we got out of the van, I realized that Cathy Barbay's mere presence in the passenger's seat had inspired me to pray. I smiled, realizing that I had experienced precisely the same phenomenon that I had come to investigate. I had been visited by an unusual, out-of-the-blue, furthest-thing-from-my-mind-at-the-moment call to pray.

Like a Bolt of Lightning Leaving

The Alleluia Community was born at a prayer meeting at a school library during the early 1970s. After intense prayer, a small group of people signed an agreement to become the type of close Christian fellowship described in Acts 2:42–47. The early founding families, many with young children, sold their homes throughout the Savannah River area and pooled their resources to buy a cluster of run-down duplexes sharing a large common pecan grove as a backyard. There, just as their role models in Acts, they soon discovered that living out elbow-to-elbow closeness in an ecumenical, social, and economic mixture was only possible with constant, daily prayer.

Then one memorable Saturday morning in 1996, God issued a prayer call beyond anything the community had ever seen. Bob Garrett, who was the music leader for the meeting where the call broke out, explained to me what had happened.

"At dinnertime on Friday, November 15, I got a phone call from my wife, Sue, who had been at the hospital support-

125

ing Cathy during childbirth. Sue said, 'Cathy has a healthy baby daughter, but Cathy's in serious trouble. The bleeding won't stop.'

"By the time I got there, twenty-five people were packed into the waiting room. We got Cathy's husband, Steve, to sit in a chair in the middle of the room, and we prayed for quite some time over him. A doctor came in, and Steve signed papers authorizing an emergency hysterectomy. After a two-hour surgery, a priest was allowed into the recovery room. He administered last rites.

"The mood in the waiting room was very serious. I thought, *This is it, we're really losing Cathy, and Steve's being left behind to raise a newborn daughter and their four other girls.*"

Bob and Sue returned home at midnight. Bob slept poorly, awakening several times to pray, "God, don't let Cathy die."

The next morning the news was bleak. Cathy had already received forty units of blood products, and the internal bleeding showed no signs of stopping. "People normally don't recover after thirty units," the community member at the hospital reported. "Even if she survives, she most likely will be disabled for life or might later die from an infection."

Bob telephoned community leader Dennis McBride to discuss what to do about the quarterly meeting scheduled for that morning. Normally, everyone looked forward to the uplifting gatherings. "Should we go on with the meeting with everyone so upset about Cathy?" Bob asked.

Dennis answered, "Maybe we should consider setting aside our usual agenda to pray for Cathy." Bob agreed, and a little before 9:00 A.M., people began slipping somberly into the gymnasium. Bob described the feeling: "The whole group was much quieter than usual, even the children, something like a crowd gathered in a funeral home. It was hushed, intense, almost fearful, as whispers went around the room. There were tears in many eyes."

After the four hundred members found seats on the folding chairs, Dennis gripped the podium and began with startling words that would be the fountainhead of a remarkable call to pray. "Friends," Dennis said, "we all know that unless God does something extraordinary, Cathy will die. But until she's dead, we're going to act and pray like she's alive."

Bob looked out over the frozen sea of faces and saw a small but perceptible change come over the crowd. The teenage boy holding the handcrafted processional cross slowly lifted it up a bit higher. A woman straightened in her chair. A man nodded. A single chair scraped as someone in the middle of the room knelt down onto the gym floor. Suddenly, without spoken instruction, the whole room was in motion as everyone got down on his or her knees to pray. Immediately the gymnasium was filled with a low hum of hundreds of whispered prayers. Bob says, "It was constant, musical, much like the sound of a chord being strummed gently on a guitar."

As the energy built, Dennis spoke. "I'd like all of the women who are pregnant or have been pregnant in the last year to come forward to stand in for Cathy as we pray." About thirty women began to make their way forward. Among the group was an unexpected face—one of Bob's neighbors. Bob said, "Apparently she was pregnant, but being such a private person, she hadn't told anyone. Seeing her stepping outside of her own comfort zone for Cathy's sake really touched me."

As the congregation prayed over the new and expectant mothers, Bob felt the energy level rise another notch in the gymnasium. After the group of women returned to their seats, various people took the podium, offering prayers, words of encouragement, and Scriptures.

Around 10:30 A.M., Bob was surprised to see a woman he knew to be shy nervously approaching the podium. *I've never heard her speak before a group,* Bob thought. *I can see her hands shaking all the way from over here, but she's coming to stand up in front of four hundred people.* The woman let out a deep breath and said into the microphone, "In the Bible it tells about a woman who suffered an issue of blood who reached out to touch the hem of Jesus' robe for healing. I think God would want us to symbolically reach out to touch the cross in prayer" (Matt. 9:20–22).

The call sent a surge through the crowd as people got up and lined the aisles for a turn to kneel and touch the cross. Bob's eyes fell on a young father holding a four-year-old on his shoulder. The man leaned toward the cross and the child's dimpled hand reached out and rested on the smooth wood. Bob said, "Seeing the child's little hand on the cross brought up more intense feelings, those feelings of childlike faith and trust that we often lose as adults.

"At about eleven, something indescribable happened. At nine everyone had come in with downcast faces; now their hands were thrust straight up to heaven. Suddenly, the atmospheric pressure inside the gymnasium just dropped, almost like a lightning bolt had left the building and traveled to the hospital. Up until that moment I had a sense of urgency to implore and to pray, and then a sudden feeling of peace swept over me. Dennis looked over and said to me, 'Did you feel something?' I nodded, thinking, *Wow! God heard us, and he's about to do something.*"

Back at the hospital, three doctors had been in worried discussion about doing exploratory surgery on Cathy, hoping to find something that could be stitched up. Dr. Cooper told Steve, "I think that your wife is going to die. This operation is just a heroic effort. Only God can save her now."

At around 11:00 A.M., the doctors opened Cathy up. They found nothing that could be repaired. They sent her back to ICU, her condition beyond any further medical help.

Meanwhile, the prayer meeting back in the gymnasium ended at noon with a no-holds-barred rendition of "Victory in Jesus" that shook the rafters. As Dennis dismissed the meeting, he proclaimed, "Go forth and pray like this always."

At 2:00 P.M., Dr. Cooper checked Cathy's clotting status and shot a questioning look at the ICU nurse. The nurse nodded. He had not misread. Cathy's platelet count had climbed back up. "Why?" he wondered aloud. "Those blood products are the same things we've been pouring into her since last night."

Although the meeting had broken up, the prayers for Cathy did not stop. Bob said, "For the next few days, every conversation started with heads bowed and hands joined in prayer for Cathy. Every mealtime prayer in the community centered on Cathy; each class period at the Alleluia School began with children kneeling beside their desks, praying for Cathy."

On Wednesday, November 20, the sixth day of Cathy's hospitalization, Bob awoke before dawn and the thought came, *Go to the 6:00 A.M. prayer meeting. Something special is going to happen.* Bob zipped his jacket in the forty-degree November predawn darkness and joined a group of about sixty teenagers gathered in a thick blanket of fog on the helicopter pad directly in front of the hospital.

The group began with a song, then they lined up and extended their hands toward the hospital in prayer. As the group formed a circle and passed the cross around to those who wished to pray, the fog around them began to turn white. With their backs toward the east, the group could see the first rays of the sun illuminating the hospital. In the twinkling of an eye, the fog vanished and a banner of clear blue sky spread out above. *God is going to answer our whole prayer, not just a piece of it,* Bob thought. *This is like the period at the end of the sentence.*

The following day, on Thursday, November 21, Steve Barbay sat rocking in a small private room in the hospital nursery, holding his infant daughter, Dora. A tape recorder was playing a tape containing a song written and performed by Cathy. The door slowly creaked opened, and Dr. Cooper entered. He said, "Steve, your wife is a little better. She's not using that much blood, her clotting is back to normal, and by some miracle she hasn't developed fluid in her lungs from the respirator. The bottom line is, I think she's going to make it."

Steve answered emotionally, "Thank you so very much, doctor."

The doctor replied, "Don't thank me. We've done nothing but watch her. This is totally an act of God."

Over the next few months, Cathy faced innumerable medical obstacles. Inexplicably, she simply got stronger and stronger as the community prayed specifically for each problem. By May 1997, six months after Cathy's ordeal had begun, she was a familiar sight in the community, out on her vigorous three-mile evening walk. Baby Dora had grown into a charming, dark-haired child. As people waved to Cathy from every door and sidewalk, they marveled at the walking miracle in their midst. A young mother's life had been spared, and a baby girl was safe in her mother's care.

And what does the name Dora mean? Appropriately, Dora means "God's gift."

The Power of the Call

It is impossible to read the account of Cathy Barbay's healing without being stunned, not only by the massive amount of blood she received but also by the massive amount of prayer. During the Saturday morning session alone, we can multiply four hundred people times three hours of prayer to equal twelve hundred hours of concentrated prayer. Yet even then we are left with the woozy feeling that we have only begun to scratch the surface. After all, the majority of prayer is done in the privacy of the prayer closet, in the silence of the heart, sometimes half a world away.

The truth is, prayer is something that cannot be punched in on a calculator, because the quantity and the quality of prayer are always immeasurable. We would be selling ourselves short to view Cathy's story as simply a confirmation of the American notion that more is always better, that the more we pray and the more prayer chains we contact, the more likely we are to get results. The measureless nature of prayer is a gift to us from a wise God who knows us quite well. He knows we would exhaust ourselves mounting personal blitz campaigns for favors for those we desperately love. Instead, God invites us to pray not as we are compelled by our own logic, passions, and fears, but rather as he quietly and firmly calls.

After concluding Cathy's story, Bob Garrett explained his own experience with prayer calls. "I've gone into the hospital room of six different people and prayed that God would heal them. All six died. Yet I'll still keep doing it, because following God's call is a mysterious thing. When I pray, I'm not trying to twist God's arm to make him do something. He loves us all. We pray as the Spirit leads, and we know that somehow, led to pray in an extraordinary way, things change and we change, even though we don't always get what we thought we were praying for."

Cathy's story is not simply a story of massive prayer, but rather a rousing tale of a massive call to pray answered by a community of people who decided one Saturday morning to break down the last barriers between each other in obedience to God's call. Bob's words to simply pray as we are called sets us wonderfully free. At last we can lay aside all worry over how much prayer is really enough and the frightening possibility that we might do too little. Whatever praying to God leads us to do will be precisely and wonderfully just right.

The surprise is again on us. We customarily see a prayer call as a straightforward, rescue/result–oriented transaction: Cathy was about to die, and God called the Alleluia Community to pray. From the throne room, however, God saw a different sort of opportunity. He not only saw the chance to heal Cathy, but he saw an opportunity to empower her intercessors.

As we shift the spotlight from the one who was healed onto the many who prayed, we find countless other stories of triumphs of different sorts: an intensely private woman publicly announcing her pregnancy by obediently going forward for prayer; another woman petrified at the thought of speaking in front of groups bringing a message that rattles the rafters; bleary-eyed teenagers up and dressed for school before dawn in order to stand in the November fog on a helicopter landing pad to pray.

Breakthroughs indeed happen as a result of calls to pray, and chief among them are the breakthroughs that happen in the lives of the intercessors. Another's crisis that touches our hearts often touches off a crisis in our own lives. Are we going to go beyond habit and comfort zone or not? Are we going to risk making a spectacle of ourselves or not? Are we going to sacrifice our plans and our time or not? Are we going to put off this call and water it down until there is not a taste of power left, or are we going to foolishly and recklessly pray for healing and resurrection and reconciliation and restoration when such things do not seem even remotely possible?

It is not always overwhelming feelings of compassion and empathy that call forth our best intercession. Rather, our best praying is often done when we experience that terrifying feeling that we are about to jump off a cliff. A bolt of lightning definitely divides the darkness in half, but we, the intercessors, are the ones sitting in the darkness, waiting for our fears to be burned up in a dazzling thunderclap of decision.

Stopped during a Walk

Since it was a clear morning, lightning bolts and calls to pray were the furthest things from my mind as I went by to see if my neighbor Pam wanted to join me on my morning walk. Pam was wearing slippers, not walking shoes. The circles under her eyes told of a sleepless night worrying over her dear friend Cheryl, hospitalized with advanced bone cancer. Pam explained that Cheryl was barely conscious, her lungs full of fluid, her heart beating furiously to keep her circulatory system working. Pam said, "I'm not walking today. I'm going to try and get an hour's rest before going to the hospital."

I nodded sympathetically and set out walking alone. As I put one foot in front of the other, a strange thought stabbed me: *Pray with Pam.* With the next footfall, I answered the rogue thought by thinking, *That's a nice idea, but I can't right now. I've got to get my walk and get right home because I have so much work to do.* I suppose after my lesson at the ball field, described in chapter 4, I should have known what was happening, but it was early in the morning and I was still not terribly alert.

And so as I walked, I allowed logic to shred up the thought. *Maybe praying silently by myself will do just as well. Instead of praying with Pam, I'll pray for her.* Unfortunately, the still small voice rattled back, *You're pretending that it's okay to change the meaning by changing one little word, but it changes everything.*

133

I cranked out the next objection. *What if Pam's already lying down on the sofa and I disturb her? Goodness knows if she's going to be a comfort to her friend and her family, she'll need her rest.*

Pray with Pam, that ridiculous thought said again. Finally I admitted my true objection. I really did not want to pray with Pam because I had never done it before and it seemed awkward. I thought, *We're not the same denomination. What if she says no?*

Unfortunately, this was a timed test, and I had to decide which way I was going to go by the time I got to the corner. There I would have to either commit myself to the normal two-mile walk or double back down the cul-de-sac to Pam's house before she went down for a rest. Either my objections were going to win or the Holy Spirit was going to win.

At the corner, I turned toward Pam's. Since I was in the midst of writing this chapter on prayer calls, I was either going to be a hypocrite, writing one thing and doing another, or I was going to have to go over there to Pam's, no makeup and no breakfast yet, and pray.

As my athletic shoes strained up Pam's steep driveway, I started a final line of fretting. *What if I pray the wrong thing? If Cheryl's dying, should I pray for healing or should I pray for God to take her peacefully?*

I finally did what I should have done at the beginning. I gave up and asked the Lord to give me the strength and wisdom to answer the call. "Well, Lord, I'm just doing it. That's all you're asking me—to do it. You're not asking me to say the perfect prayer. You just want me to be a means of bringing prayer into this situation, and here I come, jogging shorts and all."

I had only seconds between a neighbor's car pulling out of Pam's driveway and Pam's cell phone ringing to announce, "I've come over here to pray with you for Cheryl."

Pam said into the telephone something that surprised me. "Karen's just come over now to pray for Cheryl; you want to come join us?" I had the impression that the answer on the other end of the line was no, because Pam pushed the off button, took me into the kitchen, pulled out a chair, and folded her hands.

I opened my mouth and prayed. It was far from eloquent. I prayed that God would be with Cheryl and her husband and children. Then I hushed, unsure whether I should say amen or whether Pam wanted to pray aloud. After a few seconds, Pam prayed with emotion for Cheryl and her young children. Pam said amen, we hugged, and then I left. The whole transaction took less than five minutes. Overruling my objections had taken twice that long.

As I continued an abbreviated version of my morning walk, God began to speak to me again, pointing up that there are many barriers to answering prayer calls, and nearly all are inside our heads. Obedience to each call is a personal and sometime intense triumph of faith over supposed fact, trust over sight, the divine over the petty. We are often surprised by prayer calls because resisting them is usually as easy as taking the next routine step in our deeply rutted schedules and answering them is often as difficult as surrendering the last shred of our will.

The next morning Pam reported that the doctors had been able to draw the fluid from Cheryl's lungs, and by afternoon she had been able to speak to Pam. Cheryl of course still faced at best an uncertain future, yet God had used Cheryl's precarious condition to do a world of good to improve my own precarious obedience to God by issuing a simple three-word call to pray.

Praying as God Chooses

Dr. Henry "Fritz" Schaefer is a highly distinguished scientist in the field of computational quantum chemistry, but one of his greatest prayer discoveries came when his three-month-old son, Pierre, died of sudden infant death syndrome.

On the morning of December 9, Karen Schaefer went to take Pierre from his crib in their San Diego, California, home. She was horrified to find him face down in his blanket, dead. Without warning, the baby Karen and her husband Fritz had prayed for with such hope, desire, and love was dead. Pierre had been an answer to many an agonized prayer as Fritz and Karen endured infertility and the long, drawn-out ordeal of adoption. Now their whole world had come crashing down again.

After Pierre's funeral, the heartbroken couple contacted the adoption agency. "We want another baby boy," Fritz said.

The social worker measured her words carefully. "We understand how you feel. But you need time. Even biological parents have to wait at least nine months for another child. Give yourselves half a year or so, and if you still want a child, we'll put you back on the top of the list."

When Fritz told Karen what the social worker had said, they sat in sorrow on the sofa. They knew she was right. It would take time to deal with their grief, time to let God mend their broken hearts.

By June, Fritz and Karen felt they were ready to be put back on the adoption roles. They contacted the agency, then appealed to a higher authority. "Please, God, give us another baby boy," they began praying together nightly with their hearts in their throats.

In early August, the social worker called with good news. "We have a three-week-old boy for you in Eureka. The birth mother read the file describing your family and really wants you to have her baby."

The couple thanked God and went about excitedly preparing to welcome a new son into their home. "Let's name him Teddy," Karen said. "Teddy," Fritz said. "I like that."

But they were not prepared for the phone call they received from the adoption agency the day before they were to pick up Teddy. "You'll need to wait another week while we do some medical checkups."

"Medical tests?" Karen worried. "I wonder what that means?"

After a long week, the social worker called back. "We're so sorry, but it's best to forget all about that baby in Eureka. He's got too many medical problems."

The agency allowed Fritz to call the examining physician to find out exactly what was wrong with the baby. "He's basically unresponsive. Blind, possibly brain-damaged. No one's sure what's wrong," the doctor explained.

That night Fritz held Karen as she cried. He tried to soothe her. "The social worker knows what we've been through losing Pierre, and she doesn't want us to have to go through it again by giving us a baby who might not make it. She's right. It's best we just forget about this baby. We're still recovering. We'll somehow get over this, but there's a little baby in Eureka who won't. He's got terrible problems, and he doesn't even have a family."

Karen wiped her face and said, "You're right. Maybe there's nobody else who would be praying for him. Let's pray for him every night, and I'll put his name on my Bible-study prayer chain." That evening when the couple joined hands for nightly prayers, they started praying again for a baby boy and added a request that God would help the poor, parentless baby boy in Eureka.

One month passed, then two, with no word from the agency. Fritz asked Karen, "Should we use the name Teddy for another baby?"

"No," Karen replied. "It just wouldn't seem right. There's only one Teddy."

Fritz nodded. Teddy was indeed a very real baby, made real in their hearts through their nightly prayers.

One October day, Karen came home from Bible study and surprised Fritz by saying, "I've decided to change my prayer request for a baby boy."

"Why?" Fritz asked.

"There's a lady in my Bible study group who's a foster mother. She has an extra bed at her house, and today she asked us to pray for the child of God's choice to fill that bed. All along we've been praying for a baby boy. Maybe God has a girl in mind. We need to pray in a way that gives God a chance to do it his way, not ours."

Fritz agreed, and that night they prayed, "God, please send us the child of your choice." The following night, they repeated the same prayer, letting it penetrate their hearts with a new willingness to accept whatever child God might choose to give them.

On the third day, the social worker called Fritz and Karen, asking, "Can you be down at my office at four-thirty today?"

That afternoon, as the pair settled into vinyl chairs, the social worker began, "I didn't call you in here to just chat. Do you remember that baby in Eureka?"

"Of course we do." Karen answered, "We've been praying for him every day."

"Well, he's here now. He's been in town for tests. He's better. In fact, the doctors have been over him with a fine-tooth comb, and they say he's just fine." She paused and continued, "He's in the next room. Would you like to see him?"

"He's here? Of course we want to see him!" Karen exclaimed.

The couple stared wide-eyed as the baby's foster mother brought in a healthy three-and-a-half-month-old boy with dark hair and big expressive brown eyes fringed with long lashes just like Karen's. When the woman placed the baby in Karen's arms, he gazed gently at Karen and then nuzzled down contentedly in her embrace.

Karen's heart melted as tears ran down her face. "Oh, Fritz, isn't he incredible? He's no stranger. We named him three months ago, and we've been praying for him ever since."

The foster mother said, "It was the strangest thing. Over the past few weeks, I've watched this baby become more and more responsive. All I can say is that it's a miracle."

As the joyful new parents got up to leave with their son Teddy, Karen turned and asked the foster mother, "What have you been calling him?"

"Tad," the woman replied.

Karen and Fritz exchanged thankful smiles. For just as God had chosen this very special baby for Fritz and Karen, he had somehow directed both the adoptive and foster mothers to independently choose strikingly similar names for the baby.

As I thought about Fritz and Karen's story, at first glance it seemed as if their prayers were answered as they had hoped when they at last received a son. On the other hand, their answer took a decidedly unexpected turn, because the particular baby that was placed in their arms was the one that they had been prudently advised to "forget" by the social worker. But that special baby was the one that God would not allow them to forget in their prayers. In calling them to continue to pray for Teddy daily, God began binding him to their hearts before they knew they would ever be given the privilege of holding him in their arms.

In the same way, God's call to us may be to continue praying for something our minds and authorities tell us to forget. We may be called upon to revise our prayers and revise our hearts as we lay aside our choices and leave the choosing to God. God does not need our prayers to line up with what we are about to receive, but he would like us to be mentally and spiritually prepared for the wonderful surprises he is about to send.

Three February Prayers, One March Afternoon

On February 12, Margaretta, whom we first met on the ski slopes at the beginning of chapter 4, settled her children down for an afternoon nap and sat down for her daily devotions. Margaretta began praying routinely for the safety and well-being of her children, when suddenly an urgency to pray more intensely came over her. There seemed to be no rational reason to be unduly concerned, yet she found herself praying in greater and greater depth and detail that God would bless and keep her children safe. As she prayed, Margaretta felt emotions sweep over her, beginning with urgency, moving through to forcefulness, then at long last ending in a feeling of peace. After she was finished, she thought, *Wow, whatever that was I was praying about, it sure was heavy duty.*

On Thursday, February 27, Margaretta's sister Corrye was in her North Carolina home saying her nightly prayers, when a disturbing feeling—unrelated to anything that had happened to her during the day or anything she was presently thinking about—came over her. Not knowing what the sudden burdened feeling was about, Corrye determined to pray it through. As she wrestled with the sense that someone she knew was perhaps in some sort of danger, she finally asked, "Lord, who is it that's in trouble?" She picked up her Bible, thumbed through it, and latched on to these words in Joshua 9:2, "They came together to make war against Joshua and Israel."

Joshua? Corrye wondered, now even more perplexed. No one she knew named Joshua came to mind. She tried to go back to her normal prayers, but the distinct impression that someone was in mortal danger would not leave her. Finally she opened the Bible back to the book of Joshua. Suddenly she paused over these words, where Rehab requests, "That ye will save alive my father, and my mother, and my brethren, and my sisters, and all that they have, and deliver our lives from death" (Josh. 2:13 KJV).

Oh, no, Corrye thought. *It must be a family member. But who? My parents? One of my brothers and sisters?* Corrye returned to her prayers with more fervor. "God," she prayed, "please save and protect whoever it is from all danger. Keep them safe. Don't let them die."

Corrye continued her strange labor of prayer as she struggled against some unknown danger. She prayed and agonized, speaking out loud until finally the feeling subsided and she felt at peace.

The following night, Friday, February 28, two states away in LaGrange, Georgia, a friend of Margaretta's named Linda was awakened by a graphically frightful dream. She dreamed that she had been driving when she hit a little boy named Joshua. *It's got to be my son Joshua,* Linda thought in terror. *Even though I'm awake it all seems too awfully real. Is this dream some sort of warning?*

Linda tried to turn over and close her eyes, but adrenaline was still shooting through her arms and legs. She snapped on the light and awakened her husband, hastily explaining the vivid dream and the dreadful feeling that had come over her. Her husband groggily sat up, and they grasped hands in prayer. "Please, God," Linda begged, "keep Joshua safe. Don't let anything happen to him." The two prayed together until the thumping in Linda's heart finally stopped. Then she tiptoed down the hall to make sure that Joshua was sleeping peacefully before she laid back down to an uneasy sleep.

Three days later on Monday, March 3, a few miles from Linda's house, Margaretta had just pulled her station wagon down the hill into her driveway. Margaretta's two older children, Marlea, age six, and Joseph, age four, shot out of the car, eager to deliver the last two boxes of Girl Scout cookies to the neighbors across the street. As Margaretta bent to unstrap the baby from the car safety seat, a horrified scream rang out from the direction of the road. *Oh, no, our dog's been hit by a car!* Margaretta thought, her heart knocking against her ribs.

Margaretta left the baby strapped in the car seat and raced up the driveway, a prayer pulsing through her heart. At the crest of the hill, she took in the whole scene like a jerky newsreel. A fifteen-year-old girl, who was learning to drive, stood outside an open car door, screaming hysterically. Marlea was standing in the front yard, frozen in terror. About eighty feet away, Margaretta saw a small crumpled body. It was four-year-old Joseph, whom Margaretta had begun calling Josh for short.

Dizzily, she ran over to Josh, who was lying on his back on the asphalt. His tiny face was ashen and covered with blood from a gash on his forehead. Numbly, Margaretta noted Josh's sneakers lying in a nearby yard. He had been hit with enough force to literally knock him out of his shoes.

Margaretta crouched and anxiously touched Josh. There was no response from the colorless face—not a shiver, not a quiver of an eyelash. She touched his still form again, repeating one word over and over, "Jesus! Jesus!"

As horrified neighbors gathered, Margaretta looked up at them and said, "Please pray!" Someone called an ambulance, another called Margaretta's husband, another took Marlea and went to tend to the baby back in the car seat. Margaretta sat praying, "Jesus!", riveted to that spot where a small crater in the asphalt showed where her son's head had hit. Finally a small shudder started down in Josh's toes and pulsed up his body. A huge groan worked itself out of some deep place within Josh. It turned into a cry that became louder as he turned pink. "Don't move," Margaretta said. She looked up and noticed the gathered neighbors crying. "Don't worry, he's going to be okay," she said with strange conviction. "He's going to be all right."

At the hospital, the emergency staff rushed Josh in for a CAT scan, leaving Margaretta with cautionary words about extensive brain damage. But the CAT scan showed something utterly impossible. There was absolutely no brain injury. Instead, the only thing the doctors needed to do for Josh was simply to suture the skin back together on his forehead.

The doctor said, "I just can't believe this. This child isn't even bruised. Here is a forty-pound child struck by a car going thirty-five miles per hour, and we can't even tell from looking at his body where the impact occurred. There are no internal injuries anywhere, not even a broken bone, just a sprained ankle and this gash on his forehead."

At 4:00 A.M. Josh awoke, and Margaretta was overjoyed when his behavior confirmed the medical miracle. Josh blinked at Margaretta and asked in bewilderment, "Did we have a car crash?"

"Something like that," Margaretta answered, overcome with gratitude that Josh was back.

When Margaretta phoned her sister Corrye in North Carolina, Corrye exclaimed, "Margaretta, do you know how good God is?" She then told of her prayer on the preceding Thursday and concluded, "It all makes sense now. Since his name is really Joseph, I forgot about his nickname. I kept trying to think of someone named Joshua while I was praying."

Margaretta says, "When my friend Linda called and shared about her dream and how she prayed with her husband in the middle of the night, I knew without a doubt why Josh survived the accident without requiring so much as an aspirin for pain. Within days he was back, bouncing around like the active preschooler he was."

Margaretta ended her story by adding, "At church the next Sunday, the lectionary passage, which is scheduled by a master plan that runs on a three-year cycle, was Psalm 34. Every word seemed to be written just for me, especially when it said how God hears us and delivers us and not one bone will be broken [Ps. 34:17, 20]. When I heard that reading in church, I totally lost it because I felt that God had his hand on this situation, not just for a month but for some time way before."

Josh's story brings up interesting questions concerning prayer. We assume that prayer works in chronological order like the rest of our lives. A need presents itself, and we present ourselves at the doorway to the throne room with our carefully written petition in hand. But as Margaretta, Corrye, and Linda learned, sometimes something much more mysterious happens.

God disregards all notions of past, present, and future and sounds a prayer alarm over something we could not possibly foresee that has yet to happen. In the same way, God also just as easily disregards space, sometimes sending us to our knees at the exact moment a loved one stumbles into danger two states away. When we answer such prayer calls and later learn the whole incredible story, we are not just surprised by prayer, we are absolutely bowled over by prayer.

Since we are customarily the ones putting items on our daily prayer list based on the problems we know about, we seldom leave time or room for God to put other things on our prayer agendas that we have yet to dream about. Once we do, we discover a closer dependency on God, not just for the answers but also for the simple ability to pray. How can we use our intellectual powers to carefully word requests and how can we dream up likely solutions when we may not even know a single specific detail? Just when we think we are praying at our worst, having no earthly idea what to say, we are actually praying at our best, letting God have his say. For when no coherent words materialize, we must rely on raw faith that God accepts our feelings, longings, heartbreak, groanings, and agonized silences as prayers just as worthy of his ears as any poetic hymn (Rom. 8:26–27).

Who Is the One?

I was off with the family to visit our son Jeff in Colorado Springs, with a weekend trip to the ski slopes at Keystone, but I was also off on a different sort of adventure. I was writing this book, and before leaving home, I felt that something substantive was missing in this chapter. The feeling seemed to be confirmed when I looked at the page count and saw it was ten pages shorter than the other chapters. This hole in the text caused me to pray, and while praying, the thought came to me that maybe I was going to meet someone on my travels who would have a story for me. I was further impressed not to rule anyone out, particularly not those working behind shop counters to whom it would not occur to me to talk. And so I was off on a mystery tour, having to depend upon on-the-spot prayers until I recognized the right face among thousands.

On the plane, I chatted with the man next to me, and I silently prayed, "Is this the one?" *No,* a feeling inside seemed to answer. The *no* seemed odd, since we were having a fascinating discussion about how prayer had opened up Cuba to Christian clerics. My seatmate was a Cuban expatriate, his family having fled Communism when the man was a boy of fourteen. Now middle-aged, he made pilgrimages to Miami, where he took his white-haired mother to a chapel looking over the Atlantic toward Cuba to pray for the conversion of his homeland.

Are you sure he's not the one? I prayed again. The inner voice answered, *You're learning from him, especially about how there are special places of prayer all over the world where people are praying for things you don't even know about. But he is not the one.*

Once we landed and were driving to our destination, I continued on high alert. Was the Bible verse on the message board in front of the A & W restaurant in the valley my sign? I offered a small prayer, then seemed to hear *no*. Was the memo holder in the condo with a verse on it about God as our rock an indication I should investigate the owners? Another short prayer, then a *no*.

The next morning, Gordon and the boys donned ski gear for a day on the slopes. I packed a bag with a notebook and a tape recorder in case I met the mystery person in the shopping village at the foot of the lift.

I settled into a seat in a coffee shop, prayed for guidance, and noticed a woman behind me reading a manuscript. I struck up a conversation and discovered that she was a university creative-writing teacher. I asked her if she had ever experienced any unusual answers to prayer. She shook her head politely.

A lull at the coffee counter caused me to notice the two young women working behind it, so I got up to converse with them. One was from South America, and the other from Australia.

"Have either of you had any interesting answers to prayer?" I ventured.

The Australian, whose name was Diana, said, "Does 'Why me, God?' count? That's what I asked when I hit a tree while skiing on the same day last year and this year, and my knee is still messed up."

A customer came in, so I returned to my seat and prayed silently, "Is Diana the one?" and did not get a clear feeling either way. A few minutes later she came over to fill the napkin dispenser, saying, "Maybe I do have a story for you." She told how she had been skiing on a black-diamond slope in New Zealand, and as she approached an area of rocks, she began to slip. "I thought I might be able to right myself, but I was going too fast. The next thing I knew, I had fallen and was zooming headfirst right toward the rocks. I must have blacked out for a moment, because the next thing I remember, I came to on the far side of the rocks and I was no longer headfirst, but feetfirst. I looked back and saw that there was exactly one spot where there was a small gap between two rocks that formed a little U shape, and I figure I must have slipped right between them. I guess my guardian angel must have been looking out for me."

"That's amazing," I said. "Did you pray when you were falling?"

"No," she said.

I asked Diana to write down her phone number, but as she was writing, the thought came, *She's not the one, even though without a doubt angels were watching out for her. Your criteria for including a story is that someone prayed before an event happened. Maybe someone, somewhere out there was praying for Diana, but you won't be able to discover who they were or what they might have been praying.*

I thanked Diana for telling me her wonderful story. Then I breathed a prayer that God would use the telling of it to remind Diana that God cared for her.

I left the coffee shop, still not having found "the one." I noticed a number of mission-style crosses displayed in a gift shop window, but once inside, I got mixed messages from wall plaques related to astrology. I prayed, "Is he the one?" as I climbed a step toward the man behind the counter, and a definite *no* flew into my head. I turned and left the shop.

At lunchtime, I was beginning to think that I was on a futile search and had made up this whole idea. Gordon and the boys took a break from skiing, and we settled on a crowded tavern for lunch. My mind was in neutral over a hot bowl of soup when I noticed a woman who appeared to be in her fifties pull up a chair with a large party at a nearby table. Something about the woman instantly had me wondering, *Is she the one?*

No clear answer came as I thought, *I can't just go up to this woman and start up a conversation at a table full of strangers. I'll have to try to remember what she looks like in case I see her again. African-American. Glasses. Red sweater. Oh, make that a black coat. If I run into her out on the street, she'll have a coat on.*

Our check came and we left the restaurant, and I went to wandering the streets again. About two in the afternoon, I passed a tall young man wearing a huge gold cross around his neck. "Is he the one?" I prayed. *No,* came the inner reply. But slowing down caused me to notice a woman beginning to climb three steps up to a shop. The woman was in her fifties, had glasses, and was wearing a black coat, but she was definitely not the same woman I had seen in the restaurant. This woman migrated over to the handrail and was carrying an elaborately carved walking stick that looked African. Then I noticed two small crosses on a delicate chain around her neck. *Two crosses,* I thought. *That's not just hit-and-miss fashion, that's a statement.* Suddenly the inner voice seemed to say, *Go up the other side of the stairs and meet her at the top.*

When I got up the steps, I smiled and began, "Not skiing today?"

"No, not today, but I love to ski," the woman replied as she approached a shop door with another woman. Both women suddenly stopped upon seeing two contradictory signs on the door, one that said, "Open" and a smaller, handwritten one that said, "Back in a few minutes."

I took the opportunity of the locked door to ask about a tour name tag the woman was wearing. She explained that her name was Sadie, she was from Ohio, and they were with a group of three thousand conventioneers called the Brotherhood of Skiers. Her friend's name was Beverly, and she was from Arizona. Then she asked me, "What do you do for a living?"

"I'm a writer for *Guideposts*," I answered.

"Oh," she said with enthusiasm, "I read their devotional book every day. What's your name?"

"Karen Barber."

"Why, I read your devotional this morning! You wrote about a story at a ballpark. I always read the little biographies in the back, too. You have three sons."

I was stunned. I had been trying so hard to recognize "the" stranger that it had never entered my mind that the one I was to meet might recognize me. Besides, I am one of fifty writers who contribute to *Daily Guideposts*, and I have only five entries in it over a whole calendar year, making my contributions come up randomly every two months. By some quirk of fate, not only had today been my day, but this woman had been a devoted enough reader to pack the book in her suitcase and open it every morning like clockwork, something I personally had not done myself.

I blurted out, "Have you ever had an unusual answer to prayer?"

Sadie thought for a moment. Beverly piped up, "Sadie herself is a medical miracle." The woman went on to describe what an inspiration Sadie had been to her over the years, learning to ski despite her medical problems. Interestingly enough, instead of bells going off, my enthusiasm dampened as I thought, *I really don't think I need another medical story.* Nevertheless, I asked Sadie for her business card and wrote her condo phone number on it. The card made no sense to me, with prominent black letters that stood for some sort of unpronounceable acronym, "LMOLLM."

The shopkeeper arrived, unlocked the door, and Sadie and her friend went in. I went off to meet my family. I sat down at a table in the lodge locker room and asked God silently, "Is she the one?" For the first time that day, I heard *yes,* followed by the thought, *She will give you a story that you don't know about yet.*

I shot right out of my seat and rushed back to the shop. Sadie was still there. I told her I definitely wanted to talk with her, and we agreed to meet later.

In her condo that afternoon, I finally recognized the amazing story that Sadie had for me. I told Sadie, "God told me I was going to meet someone here with a story, and all day I've been chatting up strangers, trying to figure out who it was. It was those two crosses around your neck that made me speak to you."

Sadie's hand flew up to the crosses and she exclaimed, "Why, this was the only day that those crosses were outside of my sweater. All the other days they were under my ski clothes. I wasn't even going over to the shopping village today, but I had bought a bracelet and was going to keep it, but something said, 'No, return it.'"

As I was beginning to put together the series of impossible events that had lead to our meeting, I asked Sadie about what the letters LMOLLM meant on her business card.

"Why, that stands for my motto," she said, as she proceeded to explain the letters.

I stared down at the card, the chill finally going full force down my back. Here I had flown a thousand miles and had been wandering around the Rocky Mountains, praying that God would lead me to the person I was to meet, and he had shown me two crosses and had sent me up three steps to meet a woman whose business card read something I had been praying all day. What do the letters LMOLLM on Sadie's business card mean? They stand for "Lead me, oh Lord, lead me."

Just as missing pages of this chapter sent me praying and searching, we are often called to pray by the absence of things in our lives. It is the holes in our lives—those things that are missing, those things that we know we cannot obtain on our own—that issue our best calls to pray. Usually we see the holes as a deficit, not as a prayer bonanza. We pray that the holes will disappear, and we mentally mark our prayer business with mottoes quite contrary to Sadie's such as, "Save me, oh Lord, save me," or "Give me, oh Lord, give me."

It is no wonder that God launches us on adventures to places we have never been before in order to help us stumble upon the prayer formula "Lead me, oh Lord, lead me." He issues such calls to pray by the things we are missing, the things beyond our strength, intelligence, ability, and emotional energy. The moment we clearly see that we are lacking something terribly vital is the very moment that we no longer lack the vital wisdom to pray and receive God's moment-by-moment guidance.

Praying to find "the one" transformed my day from an idle day of waiting and browsing into an active day of exploration and expectation. I am thankful I knew I had more to write, because if I had not been in need, I am one hundred percent sure I never would have met Sadie. And if I had not met Sadie, I never would have had the leading prayer put into my hand on a business card, even though it was first discovered by the ancient writer of Psalms who prayed thousands of years ago, "Lead me, O LORD, in your righteousness" (Ps. 5:8).

"I Never Saw Her Face"

The television was on in thirty-three-year-old Sadie Harris-Patrick's hospital room at the Cleveland Clinic in Ohio, but Sadie was not watching it. Her eyes stared blankly at the wall, seeing only a square piece of bluish light. That was what Sadie's world suddenly looked like—objects bleeding into indistinct masses of color, people represented by moving shadows. The sign over her hospital bed read, "Legally blind. Needs assistance to get out of bed."

Sadie's troubles had begun several years earlier. One day she had been standing in her office at a trade show exhibit company talking to her boss. Suddenly she found herself sprawled on the floor. As her boss helped her up she thought in confusion, *What was that all about?* She forgot the incident until two months later when she tripped on the last step out of her house on her way to work and broke her ankle. *My goodness,* she thought, *I sure am getting clumsy.* After Sadie's ankle mended, she tripped at a Cleveland Browns football game and broke the other ankle. *I'm having a string of bad luck,* she thought as she drove to work using her left foot.

As the months went by, sometimes Sadie's legs went numb with no warning. Her sense of balance became unpredictable, and she had to hold on to walls and furniture to guard against falling. She was in and out of the hospital for tests. Then one day she opened the ledger book at work and the page was nothing but a gray blur. She squinted, stunned that she could not see a single mark on the page. She closed her eyes, waited a few moments, then opened them. She saw nothing but an underwater blur. Sadie began to panic, *I drove to work this morning; now how am I going to drive home if I can't see?*

When Sadie told her boss what had happened, he said, "You're a sick young lady. You've been fighting and pushing, but you're too sick to go on working. I'm calling the benefits office."

Down at the benefits office, someone had to guide Sadie's hand to sign her name.

Sadie's sister took her to the doctor's, and after giving Sadie a painful spinal test the doctor said, "I'm afraid you have multiple sclerosis."

Sadie shook her head in disbelief. "I can't have that," she said, thinking, *No one in my family's ever had such a disease.*

Sadie's abilities deteriorated at an alarming rate. Her mother was on a mission trip to Africa, so her sister, aunt, and uncle had to lead Sadie around, supporting her under both arms to help her walk a few steps. Finally, when she was flat on her back and could not move from her waist down, her doctor admitted her to the Cleveland Clinic.

As Sadie lay in the hospital bed staring uselessly at the television, a figure entered the room. The figure paused over the note that said Legally Blind above Sadie's bed and said in a kindly voice, "Hello. I'm Mrs. Waiter. I'm here to clean your room."

Sadie nodded and went on with her blank brooding. She saw only glimpses of movement as the woman slung a mop from side to side along the tile floor. When the woman finished, she put the mop in the bucket and moved toward Sadie's bed. Then she said something that startled Sadie. "I'm coming back tomorrow with some oil. I'm going to anoint your eyes."

"Excuse me?" Sadie asked. "You're going to do what?"

"I'm going to bring oil tomorrow and anoint your eyes and pray," the woman repeated.

Something about the motherly tone in the woman's voice sent an instant dose of trust into Sadie. "Okay," Sadie heard herself answering. Then the figure faded through the doorway, and Sadie heard the squeak of the wheels on the mop bucket fade down the hall.

Anointing with oil? Sadie wondered. *I've never heard of such a thing.* She was even less sure that praying would do any good, especially since the best doctors in the country had not been able to help her. Sadie had been taken to church as a girl by their housekeeper, Aunt Ora, but her girlhood religion had been set aside to focus on her career ambitions. She prided herself on being goal-oriented and self-reliant, in staying one step ahead of the game. It was not her style to sit idly thinking or praying. In times past when tragedy had struck, such as the loss of her only daughter to crib death or her subsequent divorce, she had handled it by keeping as busy as possible, going on, and moving on. Even now, helpless as she was, it had not entered her mind to pray. Yet something about this cleaning lady had rekindled thoughts of Aunt Ora's faith, a quiet trust that had deeply impressed Sadie as a girl.

The next morning, Sadie heard the squeak of the bucket stop outside her door, then a figure entered the room. "How are you doing today?" the voice asked as Sadie felt a pat on her hand. "I've brought the oil."

Sadie describes what happened. "She put a drop of oil on each of my eyelids, one at a time. Then she prayed. I don't remember exactly what she said, but as she asked for healing, her tone was so sweet and beautiful. She was talking as you do to your children when they're hurt or they scrape their knees. It was so soothing, so loving, so motherly. An amazing feeling just came over me. I felt peace, calmness, trust. Tears started rolling down my cheeks, and when she finished, I said, 'Thank you so much.'

"She took both of my hands in hers like this, and she was holding them so nice and tight and they felt so warm. And she said, 'You're going to be all right, baby. Just remember that you're going to be all right.'"

Sadie looked at the woman's face, but saw nothing but the same indistinct blur that she had seen for so long. "I've got to get back to work now," the woman said, letting go of Sadie's hands.

Sadie says, "As she left, I felt like that little girl again, sitting in church with Aunt Ora. I just knew that Mrs. Waiter was right. Whatever happened, it was going to be all right, even though I was still blind and I couldn't walk.

"Eight hours later, as I was staring up at the television set that the nurses had left on to keep me company, I suddenly saw the picture. Everything on the screen was crystal clear, just like before I lost my eyesight. I looked at the telephone, and I could see the numbers on the dial. Joy and happiness came over me, and I felt that God was with me.

"I rang the nurse. She called the doctor, and he came in and did tests. The doctor said, 'Your eyesight is back. But it will probably go in and out again. That's the way MS works.'

"I answered, 'Well, my vision came back, and to me, that's a miracle. God did it, that's all I know.'"

Studies do support the doctor's statement about the nature of MS. Abilities do suddenly disappear and then are spontaneously restored with no warning or explanation. But the true miracle of the call to pray does not hinge on eyesight, but rather on insight.

Sadie explains, "Being able to see wasn't the end of it, because that prayer was a turning point for me. Mrs. Waiter's prayer started me back on my journey of faith. It was ridiculous for her to stand there telling me everything was going to be all right. I couldn't even see her face. I couldn't tell if she was young or old. But she said it with such certainty and love that I never doubted."

After Sadie was released from the hospital, her sister helped her get settled into her apartment. As Sadie was being helped through the door, she thought, *Lord, how am I going to live? I haven't got a job, I can't function. I'm a grown woman, and I can't even take care of myself.* Just as soon as she thought it, a little voice seemed to answer, *Why are you worried?* Suddenly Sadie stopped and said, "I've been gone so long I've probably got mail coming out of the mailbox."

"Why don't you go later?" her sister answered. "You're tired."

"No, I'm going now," Sadie insisted. They turned around and slowly made their way to the elevator. When Sadie pulled the pile of mail out, she was astonished to find three disability checks, enough to cover her rent and her other bills. "See?" Sadie told her sister, waving the checks. "Everything's going to be all right."

Since Sadie had no equilibrium and was extremely shaky, she had to crawl from room to room. Down there on the floor, she also took her first baby steps in prayer. "God," she prayed, "I need your help, because I cannot do this by myself." Eventually she learned to use a walker. Sadie prayed for the day she could throw it away. *I have a problem, but I'm not an invalid,* she thought with determination. Eventually she graduated to crutches, then a cane. Although her mother was far away, Sadie began to pay attention when her mother mentioned that she was praying for her. *There's been a prayer safety net under me all along, but I never realized it,* Sadie thought.

Sadie took her recovery to an extreme when she went to watch some friends in a ski club take a lesson. As she sat in the lodge watching them falling all over the place and laughing, it looked like so much fun that she signed up for lessons. It took her three years to learn to ski, and since then she has skied all over the world.

Sadie showed me her walking stick and said, "My mother brought me two or three walking sticks every time she went to Africa. No one says, 'Oh, what a nice cane.' They say, 'What an unusual walking stick.' They think I'm just stylish, because I have one for every outfit. I even take it out on the dance floor with me."

As if her incredible comeback from MS were not enough, Sadie went on to tell how she had since gone through a divorce, remarriage, and then the death of her husband, Billy, in an automobile accident on his way home from work. "I had to trust God to get me through," Sadie told me.

"Then two weeks after Billy died, I found out I had breast cancer. They said, 'You have cancer, and we'll have to do surgery right away.' For some reason, I wasn't afraid. I just said, 'Okay,' as I said to Mrs. Waiter in the hospital room. Then I went to church and prayed, 'God, you take care of it.' The doctor couldn't believe it when he came out to see me after the mastectomy and I was sitting up on the side of the bed, talking on the telephone. I told him, 'God took care of me.'"

When the cancer reoccurred and she underwent a second mastectomy, Sadie trusted again. All in all, she has survived five bouts of cancer.

"I never saw Mrs. Waiter after she prayed for me that day so many years ago in the hospital, and I wouldn't recognize her if I ran into her on the street, because I never saw her face," Sadie said. "I later verified that I didn't just imagine the whole thing. She was a real person. Several weeks after my eyesight came back, I ran across a woman my age I once worked with whose last name was Waiter. I described the woman and she said, "My mother-in-law works at the Cleveland Clinic. That must have been her."

Although Sadie never saw Mrs. Waiter's face, she saw her faith with crystal clarity. So it is with all of us when we are called to pray for someone who does not yet know how to pray for themselves. We may have been moved to pray by deep sympathy and concern, but it is possible it is not the current problem God longs to fix when we pray. Perhaps he has put us on the brink of changing the future. We go ahead with our prayers as a straightforward transaction of words, never dreaming that God might be using them to give a transfusion of faith to another. As Mrs. Waiter mopped the hospital floor, she was just as blind to the future as Sadie was in the present. Mrs. Waiter had no earthly idea that Sadie would later need immovable faith not just to deal with MS but also to rebound from the death of her husband and from five cancer operations. Yet answering that call to pray changed Sadie's entire outlook on life, and with it, her future.

Many years ago, a man named Ananias heard a call to go and lay hands on a notoriously vengeful man who had been suddenly struck blind. Ananias, against his own judgment, obeyed the call and went (Acts 9:10–19). Ananias then faded into history, but the man he prayed over became the apostle Paul, who changed history by spreading the message of Christ across the whole civilized world. Paul went on to make discourses before kings and princes and to write letters that still stir our hearts today. The world was turned upside down because one obscure man obeyed a call to seek out and pray over a man whom he had never met.

Today, as we carry our daily tasks down familiar halls and into familiar rooms, let us not wait any longer to become like Mrs. Waiter. May we be like that one humble woman with a servant's name, a servant's job, and a servant's heart who changed the course of a life by quietly obeying a call to pray.

Living Out Prayer Calls

The experiences we have recounted cause us to wonder. When we suddenly feel led to fall on our knees, perhaps God intends to change more than current events. Could he be using this opportunity to send currents of power that transform us, moving us toward deeper dependence, trust and obedience?

After my experience wrestling over whether to answer a prayer call on my walk to Pam's, I wrote the following in my journal. "Here's what God is teaching me. Always answer even the slightest urge to pray." Since that day, I have tried to pray when even a weak, fleeting thought about prayer drops into my head. It has happened in the middle of a conversation on the living-room sofa, it has happened on the telephone, it has happened standing in the flower bed that divides my yard from the neighbor's. It rarely comes without my stomach immediately saying no before my mind can say yes. Luckily, my record is improving because I now know that challenging the inner barriers allows more prayer to flow through our days. And when more prayer flows, more answers come tumbling down.

Whether we are called upon to join a great community effort of intercession, whether we are directed to say a few simple words of prayer at a neighbor's kitchen table, or whether we are awakened in the dark of the night to pray for unknown dangers, power does not move until we move to simply answer the call. Although we may be continually surprised by the content and outcomes of the calls, we need not be surprised by the energy of God's lightning-bolt power that flows into our lives. May we indeed allow our rafters to be rattled as we heed Dennis McBride's parting words to the Alleluia Community after praying for Cathy Barbay, "Go forth and pray like this always."

6

SURPRISED
BY A PARTNERSHIP

*So if you consider me a partner,
welcome him as you would welcome
me.*

Philemon 17

W hen our family moved to Augusta, Georgia, and we began looking for a church, I jotted down something like a shopping list in my journal. "I want to walk into a church where I can sit back and listen and agree with the sermons. I want to be around people who believe like me. I don't want to be different." Then I scribbled an afterthought of a prayer, "Help me, Lord."

After visiting local churches, we narrowed our choices to two quite different congregations. Church number one was a stone Gothic chapel set in a walled garden among century-old oaks. An evangelism team was sent knocking on my door, the silver-haired minister preached easily outlined sermons straight from the Bible, and a tidy percentage of the church's income went to missions. Everything neatly fit my shopping list except for one small thing I had forgotten to write down. The church was located too far away from our house to drive conveniently.

Church number two, on the other hand, was just a mile from our subdivision. This recently chartered congregation was meeting in a middle-school cafeteria where the silent prayer time was interrupted by the buzz of flies. The church property consisted of a fallow cotton field with a painted sign announcing a future sanctuary. The rest of the church property—a podium, a brass cross, and some red hymnals—were hauled to the cafeteria each Sunday in plastic tubs packed onto a decrepit panel truck jokingly referred to as "The Batmobile." Most of the congregants were fairly new to churchgoing and not terribly versed in the Bible, and their children did not always behave properly during the service. Finally, although the minister was personable, caring, and an outstanding communicator, I suspected he was a bit too liberal for my taste.

After weighing the resources of each congregation, church number one seemed to win hands down over church number two. Then one Saturday, I happened to travel to Hartsville, South Carolina, near Darlington Speedway, to do a magazine article on Leland Moore, who worked on a Winston Cup pit crew. Leland turned out to be a slight young fellow with a neatly cropped beard and steady eyes that glowed with the fire of the speedway. Since I knew nothing about racing, I listened in rapt fascination as Leland explained the energizing moment he first jumped over the protective wall into the mayhem of the pit area. Through his vivid descriptions, I could imagine my eyes burning in the air, blue with overheated brakes and tire rubber, my ears split by the *yen yen yen* of the impact wrenches tightening the tire bolts.

That transformational moment of going over the wall had been beyond Leland's wildest boyhood hopes and prayers, owing to the fact that his experience with auto mechanics had been nonexistent. One day when he was grown, he gathered up his gumption and dropped by race car driver J. D. McDuffie's rural North Carolina garage and asked if he could hang around and maybe help out. Leland explained that J. D. was one of the last of the independents, doing all of his own mechanics, operating on a shoestring, and often driving on "scuffs," which are tires discarded by other high-dollar teams. J. D. never won, but he never quit. He was in the sport for the pure joy of the race.

Leland explained that as he stood in J. D.'s oily garage in the presence of the bear of a man with the bushy eyebrows, "I felt like I was asking the president of the United States for a job." Never long on words, J. D. simply nodded. And so the two began a mismatched partnership—the maestro of mechanics paired with the uncoordinated novice, the giant of a man working side by side with the ninety-pounder, the man who preferred to answer in grunts enduring the young fellow with the kazoo voice, which ran a mile a minute asking endless questions. In the months that followed, the two dissimilar men got along by simply falling into a pattern of daily work, side by side. Leland progressed from sweeping the shop to cleaning heads, then from grinding valves to being a gas runner at the track.

After hearing Leland's story, I glanced down at my watch and realized that we had talked well into the afternoon. I apologized and suggested that we go to lunch in a nearby sandwich shop. When our order arrived, Leland awkwardly picked up his hamburger. I seemed to be watching in slow motion as he struggled to aim the hamburger toward his mouth with his pencil-thin arms. He finally got a crooked bite, put down the burger, and took a swab with his napkin at the juice that dribbled onto his beard.

I sat there, realizing that I had been so taken by Leland's vivid experiences that I had nearly lost sight of the pure unlikeliness of anyone like Leland making it anywhere near a pit crew as an observer from the safe side of the wall, much less as a participant on the side where seconds count like hours. Leland had been born medically handicapped. The only thing he had going for him was a praying mother. He did not walk until age five when, miraculously, as he put it, he "just slid off the couch and walked."

That was the first in a long line of miracles—open-heart surgery at age seven, seventeen major surgeries in all. Even today, his gait was decidedly off-kilter, his hand oddly twisted. Leland had been excluded from school auto-repair courses because the counselors feared he might be injured in the shop. Although Leland was as unlikely as they come to be jumping over the wall at a Winston Cup race, J. D. had seen his willingness, his eagerness, and his dedication. In the end those loyalties had mattered more than an able body. Leland summed up why J. D. took a chance on him: "J. D. never said much about religion, but he wore a patch on the shoulder of his jumpsuit that said it all. 'Jesus Christ, the Winning Team.'"

On the long drive home, I could not shake the image of Leland maneuvering that hamburger into his mouth. I began to see that there was more to a winning team than joining up with the crew that had the high-dollar equipment, and it made me think about the choices we were considering about which church to join. I was on the verge of choosing a church based on which one had the most resources. It dawned on me that church membership is not about programs or facilities, but rather about a collective partnership. As long as such a partnership was centered on Jesus, the mismatches need not preclude a productive, heaven-sent relationship. My prayer request for some restful pew sitting and head nodding was at that instant undergoing a complete transformation, lubricated by those three simple words "Help me, Lord" that I barely meant when I wrote them down in my journal.

God indeed helped me. He helped me to discard every point of my original shopping-list prayer. We joined the nearby church with the Batmobile. I never got to warm a pew, between stacking up chairs after the service to make way for the cafeteria tables, teaching Bible school, and crusading on the church council. A year later, I was appointed missions chairperson. Since there was precious little money to send off to worthy causes, my main job was hauling junk for the missions garage sale and collecting used coats for a winter-clothing drive.

My differences in church background with the other congregants became a means for God to help me develop a healthy sense of humor and, with it, a more expansive heart. The Sunday after I had written an article on the front page of the bulletin about creating a more worshipful atmosphere by suggesting that parents limit the number of times their children leave the cafeteria during the service, I made the mistake of drinking two cups of breakfast tea before church. When it became painfully inevitable that I was going to have to make an exit for the ladies' room mid-service, I broke out in a sweat wondering how to do it without making a racket on the linoleum with my high heels. I finally reached down and slipped off my high heels and, with shoes in hand, endured the chalkboard chills going up my back as my stocking feet padded across the grit on the cafeteria floor. The ushers at the back door were quite entertained.

I found out that I was indeed more conservative than the minister the day I joined the pastor's study group. Our inaugural subject was the problem of why God allows suffering in the world. I found myself repeating what religious authorities had always said on the subject. Then the minister challenged, "But what do *you* think?" He went on to say that anyone can be a theologian and that we should examine our beliefs and be able to argue for and against them. To be honest, I had always avoided theology because I thought ordinary people like myself who were not seminary-trained scholars were prevented from having a go at it. Soon the lively discussions and disagreements in the pastor's study group were motivating me to fill page after page in my journal with thoughts, ideas, daily examples, and Scriptures about why I believed as I did.

One brilliant spring day, I walked the vacant field where a few stakes with orange flags marked where the church building would someday stand and prayed with my new friend Mary Carolyn. We wandered along the slight two-tire path ascending over a small knoll of stubble turning a sweet-smelling green in the sun. Somehow we felt that we were not just treading an old cotton field, but rather along the threshold of divine possibility, praying for a whole new crop of young families who did not yet know that they even needed a church or a God.

As we stood reverently on the knoll on the church property, dreaming and praying, I realized that God had called me to a cutting-edge partnership. Cutting edges are never comfortable places, especially when God uses the keenness to slice away some of our most stubborn habits. But cutting edges are also freeing places where exponential growth can follow the pruning. Being a member of the Batmobile church turned out to be the opportunity of a lifetime. There I grew in faith, wisdom, tolerance, and humility, not by being comfortably like others but by being quite different. Today I thank God that he disregarded my original prayer and instead sent Leland's dribbling hamburger to keep me from nearly turning down that golden partnership because of the pure unlikeliness of it all.

The Power of Partnerships

We have already discovered that when in distress, we naturally pray for God to rescue us and take away our problems. But not all problems go away easily, and some problems never go away at all. That does not mean our prayers have been unheard and unheeded. As we fervently pray for a miraculous way out of our misfortunes, God sends us a different sort of fortune in the form of a flesh-and-blood partner who will multiply our ability to cope and survive.

Partnerships are the basic building blocks of both civilization and survival. Few accomplishments can be achieved alone, even fewer times of crisis can be weathered without the sure, steady help of another. Interestingly enough, Adam dreaded the prospect of plodding through life by himself despite the fact that he was living comfortably in the eternal summer of the Garden of Eden. Apparently Paradise is simply not paradise without companionship. God made poor, lonely Adam "a helper suitable for him" long before knowledge of the horrors of sin, death, toil, and troubles had entered the world (Gen. 2:18). The same goes for us. From the beginning of our lives when we are born into a family, neither the good times nor the bad times are the right time to be alone.

As our prayers of distress reach our Creator's ears, he returns to the drawing board and sketches out a suitable person or a community of people as his answer to our pleas. Sometimes we see the genius right away, just as Adam did when he saw Eve and proclaimed, "This is now bone of my bones and flesh of my flesh" (Gen. 2:23). In the same way, some people seem cemented to our hearts right away. On other occasions, God's pairings seem more like comedic genius, looking for all the world like a Laurel and Hardy mismatch of fat and skinny, short and tall, brash and sniveling, slobby and mannered, dense and clever, simple and sophisticated.

These unlikely partnerships catch us off guard because of our own pesky expectations, that mental shopping list that compels us to seek those quite like ourselves. We look for a soul mate, never dreaming that what we may really need is a checkmate for our compulsive tendency to mold the world to our own small and confining ideas. We never imagine that someone of a different age group, occupation, background, ethnic group, gender, culture, philosophy, or temperament could be an answer to our prayers. We wish to conform. God intends to transform.

Unlikely partnerships pack far more wallop than simply getting us out of a tight spot or two. Nor does their power end with the unexpected growth that happens in our own character as we learn the skills necessary to get along and get out of our own confining ruts. Unlikely partnerships carry us to the great front steps of heaven as we stand on the marble foundation of Christianity—our astonishing relationship with Jesus Christ. Jesus says, "I no longer call you servants. . . . instead, I have called you friends" (John 15:15). We marvel at how billions of people throughout the ages have had a friendship with Jesus, given the utter remoteness of mortals having anything in common with the Immortal. The fact is, God chooses and uses outrageous partnerships in our lives as a prelude to this supremely unthinkable relationship of the temporal with the Eternal, the created with the Creator.

Of course, what goes up must come down. The Bible clearly states that our mastery of love when thrown together with diverse people is the standardized test of our true religion. The apostle John, in the midst of dealing with the head-pounding diversity of the early church, said, "For anyone who does not love his brother, whom he has seen, cannot love God, whom he has not seen" (1 John 4:20).

When we pray for help, that inch of openness can give God a mile to work. Our original request was practical enough. All we wanted was to be pulled through our current life emergency. God seizes the opportunity not only to pull us through the problem but to transport us straight through to heaven's gate using a partner so decidedly unlike us.

Drowning in Waves of Love

As I perched on a stool at Marilyn's ceramic-tile kitchen counter in her three-level McClenny, Florida, home, Marilyn's husband came in the garage door carrying an armload of groceries for a family birthday dinner for one of their four children. As he put down the bags and gave Marilyn a hug, a sparkle stole into her brown eyes. Just as I became comfortable in this small haven of domestic tranquillity, Marilyn mentioned, "It's quite a story about how we met." Then she told me how she had landed in this picture-perfect home by taking what I considered an outrageous chance on the very riskiest of partnerships. "I did it on the basis of a single prayer," she said as she launched into a story of faith-leaping nearly as high as the moon.

Marilyn's first husband, Rick, dreamed of being a lawyer but was never satisfied unless his grades were stratospheric. As a consequence, he spent most of their eighteen years of marriage taking college courses, while Marilyn covered the household expenses with her modest earnings. After a series

169

of miscarriages, they finally had two sons whose constant care doubled Marilyn's workload.

At last Rick was accepted into law school. He later graduated and took a position as a junior partner in a local law firm and got a credit card with a high credit limit to buy the trappings of success. In April 1989, after Rick had been practicing law for four years, catastrophe struck. Rick was diagnosed with cancer. Four months later, on September 17, Rick died. Marilyn was left with a pile of debts, two small sons to raise, ages three and six, no college degree, and no desire whatsoever for remarriage.

Of course, well-meaning friends suggested Marilyn remarry, telling her that she was still young. Marilyn shook her head. There was only one reason she could see to marry again—her two young sons needed a daddy. One evening, with little energy, Marilyn put together a decidedly unromantic prayer with no sugar cream icing. "Lord, I know I never asked you when I got married the first time to show me who to marry. Everyone I know who's gotten remarried who already had children has had nothing but constant problems. I want Michael and Adam to have the father you want them to have. You pick him out." Having prayed, Marilyn put the matter out of her mind.

Marilyn's strength and faith during those first few months of widowhood inspired her church. Word spread, and soon Marilyn was receiving invitations to speak at churches all over the area about how God can carry you through grief. Then one morning three months after Rick's death, Marilyn awoke feeling emotionally paralyzed. Marilyn said, "Here I'd been going around giving all of those speeches about how well I was doing, and suddenly the emotional bottom fell out of my life. I loved my children with all my heart, but the thought of getting out of bed, walking down the hall, and pouring cereal into a bowl seemed like more than I could possibly handle. I had no desire to go on living. I was afraid they were going to have to put me away somewhere because I was completely broken down."

Back in April 1989, when Rick was first diagnosed with cancer, a series of unusual events had begun unfolding at the Florida State Penitentiary. Thirty-three-year-old Allen Van Meter, serving time on theft and drug charges, sat on the edge of his cot, oblivious to the spring sunshine warming the concrete out in the exercise yard. *I might as well be dead*, Allen thought. Even from the outset, Allen's life had never been terribly promising. He had grown up in a small pocket of rural poverty where his only accomplishment was to earn the reputation of the black sheep of a family already troubled by addiction and neglect stretching back generations.

Allen did not have a job. He did not have a driver's license. The only time he had ever flown on an airplane was when he was extradited. Recently he had been diagnosed with a serious liver disease. Allen's life was over except for the burying.

Allen said, "That morning, sitting on the side of my bunk, I knew I was done with life. I looked inside myself, and everything that I had ever hoped for, wanted, or held on to crashed. I couldn't feel any emotions. I was walking around completely dead inside."

As Allen slumped on his bunk, planning ways to end his life, a fellow inmate passed by his cell. "Come on," he said to Allen, "I'm going to chapel." In Allen's zombielike state, it was easier to obey than to resist, so Allen got up and shuffled behind the fellow out of the cell block. He sank down into a seat in the makeshift chapel, his spirit still lost in the valley of death.

Then something extraordinary happened. Allen says, "I felt God's presence. I knew it was God. And he said very clearly to me, 'Allen, if you'll give me your life, I'll restore it back to you.'"

Sweat broke out all over Allen. He was startled, shocked, and utterly confused. *How could God be saying something into my spirit when I don't even believe I have a spirit left in me at all?* he wondered.

Allen said, "Yet that strange thought that God wanted me to give him my life so he could restore it grabbed on to me and wouldn't let go. I felt like I'd been floating in the middle of the ocean on a board for weeks and somebody flew by in a helicopter and dropped a ladder right in front of me. It was that real and it penetrated that much." Allen got up out of his seat and walked down front, looked the startled preacher in the eye, and asked, "How do I get saved?" The minister dropped everything, and right then and there, without a formal call to repentance except the one delivered directly into Allen Van Meter's dying spirit, he was led to the Lord.

Allen began reading his Bible. Since he had no formal religious training, he developed a straight-shooting prayer style. "Lord," he said, "I know it says here in the Bible that you forgive our sins and take them away. But are you really going to take *all* of this sin from me? And I don't understand half of what's here in the Bible. Whatever you want to tell me, you'd better speak clearly and unmistakably like you did the day I got saved."

Two weeks after his conversion, God answered Allen's prayer by indeed speaking clearly and unmistakably to him. Allen was lying on his bunk with his open Bible on his chest, thinking about his release date in September. Suddenly something happened that Allen described as "just as real as you and me sitting here. I saw something like a gold stamp that came down and rested on the top of my head. I felt God's presence again. And I heard a very clear message.

'Allen, do not get married until after February 14 and I will bring her to you.'"

Allen responded, "Okay, God. That's clear all right."

During the remainder of his prison sentence, God continued to transform Allen, assuring him that he was being delivered from the problems of his past and was being rebuilt into a new person. His liver disease improved. A few days before his release, Allen learned about a ministry group called "Just for the Love of Jesus" that offered a six-month aftercare and vocational training program for ex-prisoners. When Allen was released from prison, he enrolled in the program and checked into the center, which happened to be just down the road from Marilyn's church. Whenever a vanload of ex-offenders gathered up to attend services at Marilyn's church, Allen was onboard. The first service he attended was on September 2, two weeks before the death of Marilyn's husband, Rick.

The months wore on without Marilyn or Allen ever speaking to one another. Back at the JLJ facility, Allen told his friends about the wife God was going to bring him on February 14. On Friday, February 14, Allen walked out the door for his vocational training and said, "Okay, Lord, now where is she?"

That evening when he returned for dinner, his friends asked, "Well, did you find her?"

"Not today," Allen replied, "but the Lord told me to wait *until* February 14 and the Lord would bring her to me. I know she's out there somewhere."

On Sunday, February 16, Marilyn forced herself out of bed to take the boys to church. A week earlier, she had resigned from teaching Sunday school because she no longer had the mental energy to prepare a lesson. Marilyn dropped her boys in their classroom, but as the door closed, she was left standing alone in the church hallway thinking, *I don't know what to do with myself now.*

Marilyn's minister caught sight of her and said, "Hi, Marilyn. The guys from JLJ are coming to the fellowship hall. Why don't you come over there with me? We're just going to talk one-on-one with them and have doughnuts and coffee."

"Okay," Marilyn replied, thinking, *I guess I can handle doughnuts and coffee*. She followed the minister into the fellowship hall, where she pulled out a chair at a long table. Allen Van Meter came in and sat diagonally across the table several seats down from Marilyn. She gave him a cursory look, noting his tall, thin frame. *I've noticed him in church before*, she thought. *He seems to sing like he's so happy to be in church*.

The church member next to Marilyn asked her a question, and the minute she finished speaking, Allen started talking to another fellow farther down the table. Marilyn said, "The Holy Spirit came over me. It was like the old Star Trek shows where this force field glows around your body like a light. I was suddenly wrapped in the power of God, and I knew that something huge was taking place inside of me. I asked, 'Lord, what's going on?' As soon as I finished, love came over me like waves of the ocean, romantic love—for him—Allen.

"It was absolutely crazy. I didn't know anything about him. At that point I didn't even know his name. The only thing I knew was that he'd been released from jail, and that certainly wasn't something to recommend him. Yet I kept being swept along, wave after wave of love rolling over me. I argued with myself that this couldn't be real. Then I heard the Lord say, 'I have made you one with him.' All at once I thought, *It's him, the one I prayed about, the one who is going to be my husband and the father of my boys*.

"Well, the next thing I knew, Sunday school hour was over and the JLJ members got up to leave, because one Sunday a month they worship together at the mission center. I watched him walk out and thought, *Lord, he's leaving and I don't even know his name.* I was moonstruck, Jesus-struck.

"That night I was leading the songs at the evening service, and Allen came in and sat on the end of the pew where my little ones were. *Oh, I like that, he likes kids,* I thought. When I went to sit down with the boys, I sat in the middle of the pew between the boys and Allen. My three-year-old got sleepier and sleepier and soon he was stretched out flat on the pew and I was being scooted closer and closer to Allen. We found out later that nobody was listening to the preacher that night. They were all watching me get closer to Allen.

"When I stood up to leave, Allen said, 'Marilyn, sit down. I want to talk to you.' It shocked me, because I didn't know he knew my name. I sat down, and he told me that he was interested in me and wanted to know if I would go out for coffee with him the next night.

"The next night when we went out, we discovered that both of us had a deep conviction that God was directing us to each other. We were married soon afterward."

It was precisely here in the story that I had to ask, "But you didn't have any reservations at all about marrying him?"

Allen laughed, "I sure didn't volunteer any information to her about the details of my background."

"I could tell that his heart was sincere before the Lord," Marilyn said. "And that was all that mattered."

Few of us have developed Marilyn's deep and total reliance on God's specific guidance. At first I felt like putting a disclaimer on this story, something like that on the bottom of TV car ads in which a car careens around mountain curves, "Professional driver on a closed course." My disclaimer might say, "Only for the serious, mature Christian who knows without a doubt how to hear from God." Just as no one would advocate driving a car around a mountain curve to see how it handles, no one would advocate embarking on anything as serious as marriage without guidance, prayer, and soul searching.

On the other hand, we are drawn to Marilyn's tale precisely *because* of the story's unsettling qualities. The Bible tells us that we will know whether something is from him by the fruit it bears, and Marilyn's eleven years of marriage to Allen have certainly produced impressive results. The couple paid off Marilyn's debts and built three successful businesses from the ground up. They are faithful church members, excellent parents, and dynamic prayer partners who totally credit God for giving them everything.

But the greatest evidence of God's hand is the way he continues to work through Marilyn and Allen as a team willing to take risks on unconventional partnerships with other lost souls. I held on to my stool again as Allen launched into another outlandish story of reckless partnership. He explained that his pallet business had been plagued by a series of break-ins. After the latest burglary, Allen discovered a familiar boot print in the sawdust, which confirmed that an addicted ex-employee had been the thief who had broken in, stealing a number of five-hundred-dollar nail guns and a TV. Allen drove over to the fellow's trailer, all fired up for a showdown.

Allen says, "It was a little slum of a trailer, and he had three little kids in there. I didn't care. I was mad. I'd had the last burglary I was going to have. I said, 'Let me see the bottom of your foot.' He held up his boot and it was him all right. I said, 'You've got two minutes to get in there and get my stuff out or I'll have the police in here.'

"All of a sudden Marilyn pulled me aside and said, 'The Lord just spoke to me and said to give him a job. And give him the television set for the kids.'"

Allen laughed. "I said, 'What?' But when the Lord tells us something, we do it and we don't ask questions. We ended up paying the fellow's power bill, buying some groceries, and that same day I hired him to come work for me. To make a long story short, today the fellow's whole family are Christians, and our company has prospered like you wouldn't believe."

Few of us would dare make eye contact with a thief, much less hire him. Yet in his last human act before his death on the cross, Jesus was still putting together remarkable partnerships. He turned to the thief on the cross beside him and said, "Today you will be with me in paradise" (Luke 23:42–43). Too often when we read this story, we imagine ourselves on the wrong cross. We think of ourselves as the stable, powerful ones who are being charitable enough to take a chance on a thief. In reality, we ourselves are often the thieves, stealing divine invitations to paradise by closing our hearts to some of the unlikely people sent our way in answer to our prayers.

Fatherhood

Albert White of Sardis, Georgia, watched the rural mailbox of his former home disappear in the dust in the rearview mirror. Lines wrinkled his forehead as he prayed, "Lord, I'm not reaching my boy, Nicholas." Albert had tried to make his marriage work, and now he was trying hard to be a good father after his divorce, dropping by to see his three teenage children whenever his schedule as a power-plant security guard allowed.

As the miles stretched behind him, Albert kept talking to the Lord. "Nicholas is thirteen. In middle school. He needs a strong father. I'd tell my girls to hush in church, and to please me, they'd hush. But not Nicholas. It seems like I spent his whole schooling apologizing to teachers and cracking down on him."

Albert parked his car in front of his rental house, passed through the bare living room, and got down on his knees by his hand-me-down mattress. He threw his hands toward the ceiling, and as the tears ran down his face, he cried out to God, "Ever since my kids were babies, I've loved being a daddy. I just want to hold tight to them like that now. How am I going to be the father I want to be to Nicholas if I'm not there with him every day?"

As the months went by, Albert continued calling his kids on the phone and dropping by to see them. Afterward, he always dropped down to his knees by his mattress in longing, worried prayer. Eventually Albert met and married an elementary school principal named Nancy. Soon afterward, Albert went in for a conference with Nicholas's seventh-grade teacher.

The teacher said, "This morning when I told him to sit down, he talked back. He's so disruptive."

Albert drove straight over to his old house and called Nicholas onto the porch. "I'm not going to let you get away with being disrespectful to that teacher. You're going to move in with me and Nancy until you learn to do right."

A shocked look fell over Nicholas's face, and he started to cry. "But I don't want to leave Momma. Please don't make me."

Albert and Nancy made the necessary arrangements with Albert's ex-wife and fixed up the spare bedroom for Nicholas. That first night at dinner, things were tense around the table. Albert and Nancy tried to converse normally as Nicholas silently pushed his food around with his fork as if to say, You can force me to live here, but you can't make me like it.

Albert arranged to have a written report of Nicholas's behavior sent home weekly. Whenever Albert's shift work gave him a day off, he was over at the middle school talking to Nicholas's teachers. At first there was no change in Nicholas's behavior. A month after Nicholas moved in, he asked, "Can I go back and live with Momma now?"

"Son," Albert answered, "when you do right and obey your teachers, I'll allow you to go back."

Over the next few months, Nicholas's behavior at school improved and so did his grades. He even began to make friends with Nancy. *Finally*, Albert thought.

In May when Nicholas brought home his year-end report card, he handed it to Albert at the supper table and asked, "Can I move back home now? You promised I could."

Albert looked at the report card, then back at Nicholas in a quandary. If I let him out from under my control, what if he starts going wrong again? Albert worried. He excused himself from the table and started back toward the bedroom. Out of the corner of his eye he saw Nicholas pulling out the chair for Nancy. His heart gave a little tug. *My boy's trying hard to please me*, Albert thought. *Now I'm going to have to find the courage to try and please him.*

Albert closed the bedroom door and got down on his knees by the bed and threw his hands into the air. "Lord," he pleaded, "Nicholas is determined that he doesn't want to stay here, but it's against my nature to let him go. How can I take that chance?"

Albert anguished for a very long time, and suddenly his uplifted hands made him remember Nicholas when he was just a toddler. He would dance around and reach his hands up to Albert singing, "Daddy, Daddy. Pick me up!" That was all he wanted, just to be picked up and hugged and loved for no particular reason other than the fact that Albert was his daddy and he was his son.

God seemed to speak into Albert's spirit, "All of those times you've been on your knees, crying out to me to help your son, I've heard you and I've lifted you up, just as you used to lift up Nicholas. I'm your heavenly Father, and I love both you and Nicholas. It's the loving, not keeping a tight hold on your son, that counts. Even though you would be much happier with him staying here, your son would be happier with his mother now."

Albert stayed there with his face in the bedspread for a long time, praying, "Lord, I'm trusting Nicholas to you."

Nancy came into the bedroom with a questioning look on her face. Albert got up and said, "I guess it's time to let Nicholas go back home."

That summer, Nicholas moved back with his mother and sisters. Albert kept on praying and kept on visiting him whenever he could. In the fall, Albert nervously went in for his conference with Nicholas's eighth-grade teacher.

"How's his behavior?" he asked.

"Fine," the teacher replied.

That spring, Nicholas shocked Albert by signing up for high school college-prep courses for ninth grade. Then he passed ninth grade with flying colors. *Why, this is the kid who barely made it out of seventh grade!* Albert thought with gratitude. The next year, Nicholas made the football team and made good grades again. The change was so astonishing, Albert told Nancy, "He's done all of this on his own. The only way I can explain it is that he just 'came to himself' like the Bible says about the prodigal son" (Luke 15:11–32).

Albert discovered that even the most intimate of partnerships—that between a parent and child—must change with a changing world. No partnership is permanent. No one wants a relationship with a child to be disrupted by divorce, struggles for independence, and separate households after thirteen short years. Likewise, no one expects death, corporate downsizing, relocations across the country, or philosophical differences to force a premature good-bye. Yet even relationships that last half a century are constant only in that they constantly change. Children mature, and parents must allow them to be adults instead of children. Old age creeps in, and children must learn to parent their own parents.

The truth is, partners inevitably part. Even when we know it in our heads, it is difficult to know it in our hearts. We pray with all of our might to keep our dear ones with us, and at such times, we feel we are being ripped apart by prayer.

As we fight against letting go, we also fight disorientation and shock. We wonder where we will get that mountain of trust. How can we possibly let go of a partner who needs us as much as we need them? While we are struggling with all of our might to somehow put things back together as they used to be, there comes a moment of truth when we realize the futility of resisting the changes that have happened. Just as we are holding on as tightly as we can, God breaks in and asks, "Will you hold tightly to me instead?"

We finally stop praying against the parting and allow God to use prayer as the medicine that will help heal our broken hearts. In a breakthrough moment of sudden relationship with God, our lips finally speak wisdom to our hearts, "The happiness of the one I love matters more to me than my own. Please work the good you intend from this difficult parting." For it is there, on our knees when we lift our hands up like little children who most need a partner who will never leave us or abandon us, God whispers tenderly, "You are my own dear child, whom I love" (Rom. 8:16).

A Colt Named Spirit

On April 16, Jama Hedgecoth of Locust Grove, Georgia, nervously paced the barn as if she were about to give birth instead of the sorrel colored mare named Misty. At her animal rehabilitation center and refuge called Noah's Ark,

Jama had witnessed the birth of squirrels and rabbits, but never a horse.

"Look. Hooves!" exclaimed Jama's friend, who had provided a stall in her barn for the birth. The pair watched dumbstruck as a colt slid out and fell in a heap to the straw on the barn floor. As Misty began licking the wet, reddish-brown foal with a white blaze on his forehead, Jama thought, *Awesome, Lord!*

Jama was one of those people who dared big things for the great big God she had known since girlhood. She had signed a contract to buy the Noah's Ark property with a down payment of one hundred percent faith and zero percent cash. Luckily, she had been rescued just days before foreclosure by the last-minute intervention of a benefactor. Now that the property was paid off, Jama was chattering excitedly about jumping right in on the second phase of her lifelong vision: a home for terminally ill infants.

Misty licked the foal, but as he struggled to stand, all attempts to gain his legs left the creature with his forequarters spread-eagled on the hay and his neck lolling to the side.

They called the veterinarian, and after he examined the colt, he shook his head. "This colt was born with undeveloped chest muscles. He has to be able to stand in order to nurse and for his lungs to work properly. Besides, he's got a fever and an infection." He paused and said, "You may have to take a hard look at all of the options."

Jama answered firmly, "You know I'm adamant about not putting animals down. The only option I want is to know how to get muscles back in his chest so he can stand up."

With characteristic determination, Jama enlisted her friend in the awkward task of trying to hold the colt up under his mother's belly so he could nurse. Unfortunately, the mare sensed there was something dreadfully wrong and nipped Jama's arm, leaving a nasty bruise.

The veterinarian suggested, "You could try bottle-feeding that colt, but you'll have to get special milk."

"Okay," Jama said, "that's what I'll do." She loaded the colt into the back of her van and drove toward her small ranch house on the Noah's Ark property. As she drove, she glanced back at the colt all sprawled out and thought with dismay, *He looks one step away from being buried.* Suddenly the colt picked up his head, looked at Jama with inquisitive eyes, and let out a soft whinny. Jama's heart stirred, and she began to cry as she told the colt, "Watching you try to get up, I can tell that you're as determined as I am. Your name's going to be Spirit, because you're going to make it."

When Jama arrived home and carried the colt into the donated tent set up in front of their small house, one of her teenage sons questioned her, "Do you know how much milk he's going to drink?"

Jama gave a dismissive nod. She knew well enough how many mouths there were to feed in the household, including Jama's husband, four teenage children, and the five displaced teens they had taken in. Then there were the cages full of baby animals being bottle-fed—abandoned squirrels and rabbits, even a blind llama. Jama knew they could ill afford the milk, but giving up on the colt did not even vaguely enter her mind. "Go get the others and we're going to pray," she told her son.

Jama's family gathered in the tent around the colt and joined hands. Jama's father, an itinerant evangelist, spoke while everyone else joined in silently. "We need a miracle for this colt, Lord. Not just a little miracle; we need a big one. Totally heal him. Yet not our will but yours be done."

Spirit sat there listening to the human voice, his head cocked in attention. As the group left, the colt tried to struggle to his feet to follow them. Jama's heart just broke, and she ran back to hold him. "Poor little Spirit," she said, "you know that if you don't stand up, you'll die. But I can't be picking you up when you're all grown up and a thousand pounds. You've got to learn to walk; you've just got to."

Jama fell into an exhausting routine of bottle-feeding the colt. Her brother went to feed stores, begging for donations of damaged milk packages. Jama found herself getting out of bed every two or three hours to feed the colt. Finally she fixed up a pallet in her bedroom for Spirit, using a sleeping bag with a plastic garbage bag under him for easier cleanup.

Desperate for any kind of advice she could get, Jama telephoned an orthopedic surgeon who had treated her husband a few years earlier.

"I'm not trained on horses," he told her. "But you might try the same kind of physical therapy that works for human infants. Four to six times a day you need to move his legs up and down, make sure you're standing the horse up even if he can't stand on his own. Massage him. Make sure you keep him moving."

So Jama embarked on a round of horse physical therapy, carrying the colt out to the tent during the day, where he was rubbed and exercised, then back into her bedroom at night, where his soft, musical whinny would awaken her for his feedings.

When more problems developed, Jama doggedly developed more novel solutions. Spirit began getting sores on his knee joints from thrashing around trying to get up. A trip to the thrift store produced old socks. The sock feet were cut out and sleeves made to slip over Spirit's hooves and onto his knees. Finally a volunteer sewed a pair of "pants" for the horse. Other open sores developed. The orthopedic surgeon donated brightly colored bandages to wrap the colt. Jama laughed at the neon "mummy colt" all wrapped up for protection.

Every moment Jama was working with Spirit, she prayed ardently for his healing. She asked all of the volunteers to be in prayer. She put Spirit's name on church prayer chains. Jama told God, "You know, Lord, when I was about to lose this property, I was praying matter-of-factly, because if you didn't want me here I could be just as content ten miles down the road somewhere else. But this is different. This is life. Spirit has a beating heart, and he's connected to my heart by love now. I'm the only momma he's ever known. I'm begging you. Please, please let him live. Let him stand up."

Little by little, Spirit began responding to the therapy. His appetite improved, and he was gaining several pounds a day. Then when he was three weeks old, Jama lifted Spirit to his feet and slowly withdrew her hands. He wobbled a moment and stood on his own. Jama went flying all over the farm, spreading the good news. A few days later, Jama was singing in the fields with her hands thrown toward the sky when Spirit ventured one tiny step before falling.

Jama was ecstatic, but she also had a nagging concern in the back of her mind. "He's getting heavier," Jama told her office manager. "We're not going to be able to carry him around much longer."

"Why can't we design some kind of a walker for Spirit?" the office manager suggested.

"That's a great idea!" Jama replied, never minding the fact that such a thing did not exist. Jama's brother took on the challenge of finding a metalworking company willing to design and build such a contraption. Most businesses owners replied, "Let me get this straight. You want a walker for a *horse?*" Finally a company called Metalflex in McDonough, Georgia, which designs and builds metal chairs and tables for fast-food restaurants, volunteered to give it a try. They incorporated four bicycle wheels onto a metal frame with a belt designed to strap under Spirit's belly for support.

While the walker was being built, Jama remained confident. She tried to ignore the fact that Spirit had good days and bad days and the bad days were starting to come more frequently. She felt certain that once he got up in the walker, the fluid would clear from his chest. She was sure that the love and care they were lavishing on him would help heal the colt who wanted to walk as desperately as Jama wanted him to.

Two days before the walker was to arrive, the donors who had purchased the property for Noah's Ark came for a visit. Jama excitedly told them about the colt who was going to learn how to walk. The woman asked, "What are you talking about?" It happened to be a cold rainy day, and Jama had kept Spirit bedded down in his sleeping bag in the bedroom. Jama opened the door, and when the woman saw the five-week-old colt lift his head and let out a small whinny, tears started running down the woman's face.

Several days later when the newly invented horse-walker dubbed "The Spirit of Noah's Ark" was finally ready, an enthusiastic audience of family and volunteers watched as a small red colt was strapped into the contraption. He stood with a questioning look on his face, then dug his back legs into the grass. The walker shuddered, then moved forward a few feet. Everyone clapped, cheered, and cried.

The next day, Jama received a telephone call from her benefactors. "Jama," the woman said, "we want to build you a house."

"A house?" Jama repeated, "Like a home for terminally ill babies?"

"No, Jama," the woman replied, "a personal family home. Your family sacrifices so much for your dreams. No one should have to share their bedroom with a horse."

"We don't need much, just a double-wide trailer," Jama stammered.

186

"No. Hire an architect and tell him what you want," the woman insisted.

Two days later when Spirit came down with another grave infection, Jama was still grappling with the woman's offer. Why would the Lord have this woman offer her a family home when she was praying with all of her heart about building a home for terminally ill babies?

In the middle of the night, Jama found herself praying as she gave the listless colt his bottle, "Please, Lord, just let him finish this milk up." As she thought about the home for terminally ill babies, she had imagined every detail in her mind—the bright pictures on the walls, the cribs with soft blankets, the rocking chairs. But one scene had always troubled her. She pictured herself sitting in a sunny nursery, rocking a baby who was about to die. Try as she might, she never could imagine how she would ever be able to let that baby go. Letting go was totally against her nature. She always dreamed big and prayed big. How would she ever have enough faith to let a baby die? It seemed absolutely impossible.

Suddenly, Jama looked down at the weakened colt and realized, *This is the baby you've imagined yourself rocking. This colt is going to die. He's going to challenge you. Are you going to allow God to take him back?*

Jama cried back, *There's no way I can do it. I'm putting in ten hours a day to make him live. I'm sacrificing my sleep. I'm praying every minute. Everybody is praying and hoping and believing. What if I can't let him go? What if I fall apart?*

Over the next few days, Jama found herself begging for smaller and smaller miracles for Spirit. "Lord, just let him talk to me. Just one more little whinny. Lord, let him swish his tail." At the same time, she just as ardently began praying a larger miracle for herself, "Lord, you've got to get me ready. The time is coming too fast. Hurry and change my

187

heart so I can deal with this. The kids are looking at me.
The volunteers are watching my response. I certainly don't
want to stand up and stomp my feet and act like a baby
and ask why did he have to die. But that's how I feel. I've
got to grieve."

Saturday, May 23, dawned warm. Jama gathered Spirit
in her arms and carried him out to the tent and laid him in
the straw and tucked a worn blue blanket over him. Then
Jama sat down and put the colt's head in her lap and began
talking to him. "I have to release you, Spirit," she began. "I
know you're not human, but talking to you helps me. I think
I'm ready. Will you help me?"

The colt's dark gentle eyes stared back softly, and his labored breathing seemed to ease. Jama put her head down
on his neck and cried. As she cried, she prayed, "God, you
know you gave Spirit to us, and I know you can take him
back because he's yours. But you've got to do something
inside of me so I can release him. You've got to fix me, help
me understand the big picture. Why did you allow me to
have him just for a while, when you have the capability of
totally healing him?"

All of a sudden, God seemed to send an answer into Jama's
mind, "My plan is bigger than yours. You have to learn to
accept. You have to learn to love and then to let go."

Jama buried her hands in Spirit's warm mane, suddenly
seeing the work that Spirit had been sent to do. In his short
life, he had touched many lives. Volunteers who had not set
foot in a church in years had been praying for Spirit. The
displaced teens, who at first had seen the colt as a bother,
had been changed. Now they begged to feed him or take
him out for his therapy. But more importantly, God had used
Spirit to do a work in Jama's own heart.

"I see what you're saying now, God," Jama said, wiping
her face. "I'm not emotionally ready to work with terminally

ill babies. I thought I was, but I need more time to prepare. You're showing me that you'll help me, that eventually I'll be able to do it. Help me be more willing to accept your plans instead of mine."

As Jama got up to leave the tent, Spirit stopped breathing.

Jama's husband and sons dug a grave up near the house, painted a big rock from the field white, and put it on the grave to mark it. Then they held a family memorial service, thanking God for the five weeks Spirit had lived with them.

Slowly a new plan formed in Jama's mind, one that she had not considered before because her heart had been so firmly set on opening a home for dying babies. Jama met with the architect and had him draw up a ranch-style ten-bedroom home with ten bathrooms and a large screened porch.

Three months after Spirit's death, Jama's husband drove up and said, "Honey, there's something you've got to see." Jama jumped into the truck, and they rumbled out to the field. There in the field was a bay Arabian horse named Annie, with a dark mane and tail. And there, nursing her, was a little reddish brown foal with a star on his forehead. "No way!" Jama exclaimed. "I know you said you thought she was getting fat, but we just thought she was eating too much!"

As Jama petted the healthy foal's warm, rich neck, tears ran down her cheeks. "He looks so much like Spirit. Isn't it neat that God sent us Spirit to teach us and then gave us this foal to love and treasure?"

When Jama's new ten-bedroom house was finished, her family moved in, and so did the first of many foster children that the new modern house could accommodate. Instead of nurturing dying babies, God had changed Jama's prayers and plans. He wanted to use her compassionate heart to start working with children who would have a chance to live and grow up into emotionally healthy adults with the unique care they could only get at Noah's Ark. Where else could children with damaged emotions nurse baby squirrels and befriend three-legged dogs and lose themselves in caregiving so that they themselves would again learn how to trust and love and grow?

The most mysterious part is how God used a single glimpse of Spirit in a sleeping bag on the bedroom floor on that cold rainy day to loosen the heart of Jama's benefactors to offer to underwrite a new home. In God's wonderful economy, a stricken colt provided both the vision and the wherewithal to make it come true. Because there once was a foal named Spirit, Noah's Ark Children's Home exists today.

Jama's story points out to us that partners do not always have to be human to be sent by God. Sometimes the most powerful miracles happen through our relationships with other living creatures. In animals we see qualities we need to develop, such as loyalty, trust, acceptance, determination, and joy (Prov. 30:24–31). Animals invite us to accept ourselves in the same natural way that they instinctively accept us. And when we speak to animals, although we know they do not understand our words, we get the feeling that they somehow understand the inner *us*. Animals also give us experience being keepers, masters, and caregivers so that we might better understand how our Master cares for us.

More importantly, our partnerships with animals help us call into question our notions about the usual hierarchies in all of our relationships, human and otherwise. Jesus says that often those we consider the least among us are really the greatest (Luke 9:48). Will we dare to turn our world upside down, joining ourselves to those a few rungs or a hundred rungs below us? In the past, we have reached down with the thought of rescuing someone below. Now we know that in so doing, we are really rescuing ourselves from our own narrowness. God can use the parishioner to minister to the minister, the employee to lead the boss, the pupil to teach the teacher, the child to help the parent grow.

These role reversals of powerful and weak, masters and beginners, kings and commoners, send the sweeping refreshment of God's Spirit into our lives. The cost on our part is to at last lay aside our foolish pride concerning position and power structure. The Bible says, "Whoever welcomes one of these little children in my name welcomes me; and whoever welcomes me does not welcome me but the one who sent me" (Mark 9:37). And so, in welcoming partnerships with the very smallest of the small and the weakest of the weak, we suddenly become strong enough finally to love.

Living Out Partnerships

As we lift our prayers for help and wait expectantly for an answer, God may be at this very moment hard at work sketching out a partner who will help us through our difficulties. We may recognize our intended partners by the comfort, relief, and encouragement they bring, or we may at first refuse to acknowledge them because of the chaos and unsettling changes their presence flings into our lives.

In either case, it is only after traversing much time and many difficulties together that we finally discover God has answered our prayers by sending us something more excellent than rescue, help, encouragement, or companionship. Through our partners, we have struggled toward intimacy, toward knowing and being known. We at last lose our taste for sugar-cream relationships and fully embrace the kind of love that "bears all things, believes all things, hopes all things, endures all things" (1 Cor. 13:7 RSV).

As we look for the one unexpected face in the crowd, we are really looking for that unbreakable love that Jesus called oneness. Every time two suddenly become one, or five hundred become one, as happened at Pentecost, a single prayer is finally being answered.

Two thousand years ago Jesus prayed, "That all of them may be one, Father, just as you are in me and I am in you" (John 17:21). Today may his prayers continue to be remarkably answered in our lives as our world shrinks slowly into oneness.

7

SURPRISED
BY SCRIPTURE

All Scripture is God-breathed and is useful. . . .

2 Timothy 3:16

I moved slowly down the aisle of the thrift store that November day, wondering if God would ever speak to me again. The thrift store is my favorite place to escape from my problems, a place where I can always find something worse off than myself to rescue—maybe a piece of rhinestone jewelry with a broken clasp, a tarnished lamp base begging for a new shade, a piece of green crockery from the fifties in need of an admirer.

The problem I was running from that particular day was not a pretty one. A week earlier I had telephoned a woman to ask if she might be willing to share her story with me. The woman replied, "I'm sure if you've prayed about it, it's fine."

"Yes," I answered. Actually, I did not exactly remember formally praying about asking her, but she *had* come to my mind several times. Surely that was practically the same thing.

But that night at a church meeting as I sat with my eyes closed and my mind in neutral while our leader prayed over the usual list of ill and bereaved, the thought came to me, *You lied. You didn't really pray, now did you?* I squirmed, thinking, *I suppose I didn't.*

An uneasy week passed while awaiting a return call from the woman. When I finally reached her, she said, "I've had a knot in my stomach for days because I hate to say no to anybody. But I just don't feel sure about this. I want God's will to seem perfectly clear without second-guessing, 'Did I do the right thing?'"

I swallowed and agreed with her that we should abandon the interview idea. I hung up knowing I had been caught red-handed and red-faced by the Holy Spirit. Not only had I been sloppy about praying, but I had compounded things by lying about it. I sank down at my desk and wrote in my journal: "Lord, here I am botching things up because of my lack of prayer. Help me to be a good steward of the opportunities and responsibilities you've given me."

So there I was in the thrift store, worried and depressed, needing a sign from God that despite my shortcomings, he was still willing to work with me. I moved down the jumbled shelves of dishes and glassware and started rummaging through a pile of discarded pictures, hoping to find a vintage frame. I was ready to toss aside one particular picture in a cheap, plastic frame, when my eyes met a colorful Bible scene. I curiously turned it over. The page notations on the back indicated that it was an original watercolor illustration made for a children's Sunday school guide. Unfortunately, there was no caption or Scripture citation explaining what the painting was meant to illustrate.

I turned the picture back over and studied it. A group of men were sitting waist-deep in a field of multicolored flowers. Christ was standing with his back to the viewer with his hand stretched toward the sky, where a flock of birds was soaring over a mountain range. There was something unusually soothing about the picture, almost as if you could sit right down in the flowers and feel the brush of the breeze against your cheek.

I counted out a few dollars for the picture, brought it home, and propped it on my desk. As I stood back to admire it, suddenly I thought, *Mountains! Maybe it illustrates something from the Sermon on the Mount.* I found the passage in Matthew and paused over the part that tells how flowers do not spin nor make clothes, yet they are splendidly clothed, how birds do not sow nor reap, yet God feeds them. Jesus explains, "If that is how God clothes the grass of the field, which is here today and tomorrow is thrown into the fire, will he not much more clothe you, O you of little faith?" (Matthew 6:30).

Thank you, God, I thought with a smile. *Even when I had little faith and even less faithfulness, you set that illustration on the thrift shop shelf, waiting for me to find it. Most of all, thank you so much for speaking to me again. This Scripture reassures me that despite my mistakes and shortcomings, you will continue to provide.*

I pulled up my desk chair to the computer, newly comforted and eager to get back to work. Then, as I typed a few words onto the screen, I was struck by something terribly strange. *Isn't a Bible passage made up of words printed on paper with ink?* I thought. *Isn't Scripture something you read in a big black book?*

I gazed in astonishment at the colorful picture, suddenly glimpsing the vibrant God behind it. Even though I could now easily read a powerfully comforting Bible passage written all over my thrift shop treasure, there was not a single word printed on it.

A Living Book

This chapter is about the powerful prayer answers that tumble into our lives when Scripture suddenly becomes pageless and inkless. It is about how God's written Word stops being history and turns into our story, colliding with our hopes, needs, and shortcomings. Receiving such prayer answers is not about our opening up the Bible so much as about the Bible opening us up, meddling and mending, soothing and sowing, convicting and compelling.

At first, being surprised by Scripture seems as contradictory as being surprised by prayer. After all, we study the Bible as a guidebook for daily living, and we fully expect to find answers within its pages. But this solid reliability causes the same amnesia that we often experience concerning God's presence. Since the Bible can be propped up on a shelf like any other book, we fail to recall how extraordinary it is in the same forgetful way that we fail to note the unseen force called gravity holding the book down to the shelf so it does not fly randomly around the room. The Bible is one of those right-before-our-eyes miracles, so implicit that God sometimes must work unusual circumstances to make the Scriptures explicit enough to us again to let their glory dawn anew in our hearts in answer to our prayers.

The simple act of finding just the right Bible verse in our daily reading or hearing a needed Scripture quoted randomly at a meeting is absurdly improbable. How could we possibly open a fourteen-hundred-page book composed of roughly twenty-eight thousand verses that are not consistently arranged in any topical, historical, or logical order and suddenly stumble upon exactly what we need? Yet this happens day in and day out with little notice until someone wakes up and again hears the very voice of God.

A Scripture for Superman

Home-builder Gary Garner earned the nickname Superman the day he glanced up at a twelve-foot-high piece of elm paneling in a great room under construction and told his carpentry crew, "They're off-level an eighth of an inch at the top." The incredulous carpenters got up on their ladders with a level. Sure enough, the bubble nosed just over to the one-eighth mark.

When Gary instructed them to redo the whole room, they dubbed him "Superman" because he required everything to be superhumanly perfect.

Gary could not explain how he had seen that slight deviation; he simply had an uncanny eye for mentally fitting things together. He had been trained by twenty years as a furniture builder, and every house he built was a masterwork, fitted together as precisely as a fine piece of furniture.

During the 1970s, there were plenty of other builders with less talent reaping the financial rewards in the exploding suburbs north of Atlanta. Gary launched his business with some borrowed cash and the heady buzz he felt when people "oohed" and "aahed" when they walked through one of his houses. He drove a new, high-powered Dodge Charger and lived in a four-bedroom, three-level Williamsburg-style house in a swim-and-tennis-club neighborhood with his wife, Nancy, and their four children. Gary called it the golden ghetto, but the upscale living and the nickname Superman suited his perfectionist, in-charge sense of pride.

Then in 1974, when interest rates hit fifteen percent, qualified home buyers willing to pay for the kind of quality Gary produced disappeared, leaving him sweating out the construction loans on two unsold houses. One day Gary picked up the mail from the kitchen table and paused over a letter from a legal firm. Nancy turned from the stove and asked, "What is that?"

"Oh, nothing," Gary answered. He winked and then went to his basement office and opened the letter. Inside was a notice of a lien placed by an unpaid supplier on one of Gary's houses. Sweat formed on Gary's palms, but he told himself, *Calm down. They'll get paid off when the house sells.* Gary stuffed the notice back into the envelope and put it in his bottom right-hand desk drawer. A year went by, and the drawer got fuller and fuller. One house sold, but the other did not. When creditors started flooding Gary's answering service, he quit picking up his messages.

One day in 1975, Gary looked up at a center cedar ridge-beam in a great room in a home he was building. He paused and waited for the angle at which the rafters would merge from each direction to slip into his mind. Nothing came. Absolutely nothing. Gary thought dizzily, *What's happening to me? It's always been right there in my mind when I'm trying to figure out how to do things. I've always been in complete control. I've always relied totally on my own talents.*

Finally, at eleven one night, a contract came through on the last house Gary was carrying. *Maybe I'm out of the woods,* Gary hoped as he unfolded the papers. The figure shot off the page like a bullet hitting him right between the eyes. The offer was incredibly low, almost insulting. *There's no way I can accept this,* Gary thought numbly. *I owe thousands more on that house than this!*

Gary tried to calm his burning stomach by watching the late show. He crawled into bed exhausted. Sleep never came. Night after night he could do nothing but toss and turn until the blankets were twisted. A voice inside Gary's head kept saying, *You're a failure. You're dying, and Nancy doesn't even know it.*

More notices concerning lawsuits and judgments arrived. His checking account was garnished and overdrawn. Finally Gary went to a doctor, who prescribed a tranquilizer before bedtime. Soon one tranquilizer was not enough, and Gary was taking two. Even at that, Gary only slept for a couple of hours. He got out of bed in the morning aching as if he had been beaten with a hose. He lost his appetite, and his weight began to drop.

One morning as Gary listlessly drove to the construction site, he approached a bridge abutment. An insidious voice went through his mind: *You're not Superman. You're a failure, and you've never done anything good. Your family would be better off with your three hundred thousand dollars in life insurance money. At least then your daughter Sherre could go to the university and your debts would be paid off. You're worth more dead than you are alive.* As Gary neared the bridge, he crossed his hands over the steering wheel lest he unconsciously obey his unsettled mind. *God help me,* he thought desperately.

When Gary got home that evening he told Nancy, "Remember that priest who invited us to a prayer meeting? Isn't that tonight? You acted like you wanted to go. I'll go if it will make you happy."

When Nancy and Gary arrived at the church, the pair self-consciously took seats in the back row of the circled chairs as several men tuned guitars. Sitting there, Gary looked more like someone suffering from a consuming disease than Superman. As the others began to sing, Gary crossed his thin arms and stared intensely down at his feet. His posture warned, *I really don't need whatever it is you think you have.*

When the singing stopped, the fellow directly across from Gary broke open his Bible. The limber leather binding seemed to fall open of its own volition. The man did not so much as turn a page, but rather looked right down and read the first verse that his eyes fell upon. "Unless the Lord builds the house, those who build it labor in vain," the man read (Ps. 127:1 RSV). Then he closed the Bible.

Gary says, "I tried hard not to fall out of my chair. It just blitzed my brain. He just broke open the Bible, read it, and shut up. I wondered, *How does that guy know I'm a builder? How does he know I'm working like a dog and getting further and further behind? How does he know I'm dead all over?*

Despite his skepticism, during the next week, Gary found himself wondering about that unusual Bible verse. There had to be a gimmick. Yet try as he might to figure it out, Gary knew that the man had nailed him. During every sleepless moment on his wrinkled sheets, his weary body whispered, *Yes, it's all in vain, just like trying to sleep with your nerves tied up in knots.*

On the next Thursday night Gary announced to Nancy, "I'll go back to that prayer service just to please you."

Once at the prayer meeting, Gary again crossed his arms, scowled, and doubted. But when he left, he thought, *Whatever they're doing, it's working. They're happy and joyful. They're into something that just might be my answer.* By the third week, Gary realized, *Going to this meeting is starting to get me through the week.*

In the sixth week, after the meeting had broken up and most of the group had departed, Gary blurted out, "Would you people pray that I can sleep?" He bit his lips, barely sure he had actually asked such a preposterous thing. Nancy added, "He hasn't slept well in months."

Gary said, "Quick as a shot, they sat me down in a chair, and they put their hands on my shoulders. They began to pray that I be healed and that I would be able to sleep at night. They were all whispering and praying together. I felt a whoosh, like a jet was right under my chair. I almost opened my eyes to see if we were going through the ceiling, but I figured even if we were, it was all right because something good was happening that I couldn't describe. It was the best I had felt in months."

The group prayed over Gary for ten minutes. As they left the church, Nancy reminded him, "Don't forget to stop at the drugstore for your tranquilizers to help you sleep."

Gary answered, "If we believe that God heard those people's prayers, we're going to have to give it a chance to work. We'll wait till tomorrow to fill the prescription." (Note: It is never advisable to abruptly stop taking prescription medicine without consulting a doctor. Because Gary was prescribed the tranquilizers on an "as-needed" basis as a sleep aid, skipping a dose was permissible.)

At eleven o'clock that night, Gary climbed into the bed, pulled up the sheets, and lay very still, waiting for something to happen. Then he closed his eyes. He says, "Boom. The next thing I knew, my eyes popped open. I was looking straight across the bedroom, and a blinding ray of sunlight was bouncing off the mirror. I blinked and looked at the clock. 8:00 A.M.! I could see a patch of brilliant blue sky through the window, and the songbirds sounded like they were trying to get into my room to sing to me. I hadn't even noticed before that it was April. I looked down at the covers. They were straight. I hadn't moved an inch all night.

"The whole experience at the prayer meeting the night before came back to me, and suddenly I felt like I wasn't in the room by myself. The Lord's presence was there. I thought, *If the Lord can do this, he can solve my problems. I need to do whatever he says.*

Gary got up, went off to work, and told his carpentry crew how he had been prayed through the ceiling and then had slept like a log. They thought he was crazy, but whatever craziness it was, it had changed Gary.

That evening Gary went down to his office, sat down at his desk, and slowly pulled open the bottom right-hand drawer. He took out every lien and judgment and laid it on the desk. The words of the Scripture came back, "Unless the Lord builds the house, those who build it labor in vain." *Now I understand that verse,* Gary thought. *If you don't have God working in your life, you're a disaster waiting to happen because you're relying totally on yourself. And when you fail, you're ruined. It's my own stubborn pride that caused me to bury these debts and stuff my problems until they've nearly eaten me alive. It's time to let God start doing the building, not Gary.*

Gary went back upstairs and came clean with Nancy about their whole dismal financial situation.

"I wasn't sure what was wrong with you," Nancy said. "At least we can talk about it now."

Gary replied, "I've decided not to run anymore. I realize I'm a perfectionist, and I couldn't admit that I was in trouble. I'm going to start answering my calls; I'm going to start being open and honest with my creditors instead of hiding out. I'm afraid we're going to have to cut back on things here at home. We don't have the money for Sherre to go to the university. I'm so sorry. It's going to be tough, but I know the Lord will bring us through."

"We'll be all right," Nancy said.

Things were soon turned upside down in the suburban household. The swim-and-tennis-club membership was dropped, and Gary and Nancy began practically living at prayer groups and Bible studies. Sherre attended community college and later went on to pay her own way at the university. Gary ultimately got out of the contracting business in 1979 when two withdrawn three-hundred-thousand-dollar contracts put him out of business, but he saw it as a godsend. Gary's faith had grown by such leaps and bounds that he said, "I wasn't fearful. I just knew that the Lord was leading me into something else."

I met Gary and Nancy on a Sunday morning nineteen years later, when the church congregation mentioned in chapter 6 finally moved from the school cafeteria into our first building. Gary was the artisan commissioned to make the lectern, the communion table, the altar rails, and the magnificent wooden cross suspended from the sanctuary ceiling. When the minister explained how the mahogany communion table had been designed with curving, graceful supports underneath that suggested the underpinnings of a bridge, symbolizing how Jesus has bridged the gap between us and God, I felt awe spread over me. Gary Garner had gone from trying to be Superman to letting God's Holy Spirit work supernaturally through him. Instead of putting people into houses, Gary now puts God into people's houses and churches through his woodworking business called "Images of the Cross." In fact, it was one of Gary's handcrafted crosses that the Alleluia Community reached out to touch as they united in prayer for Cathy Barbay in chapter 5.

It is amazing to look back and see how a new man, a new family, and a new career were built because of the living power of a single verse of Scripture read at random by a stranger to no one in particular. Often we, like Gary, hide out on the back row of skepticism and despair, able to only make a halting, last-ditch prayer for help that we barely expect to be heard. The last thing we think will happen is that we will be answered by having a single Scripture nail us and make our hearts burn within us (Luke 24:32). The last thing we expect is to be converted, to be made new, to begin the first day of the rest of an incredibly blessed life.

Shatterproof

It was a quiet Monday morning in August 1981 at Ramstein Air Force Base in Germany. Just after seven o'clock, the morning sun was finally beginning to seep through the glass-brick window a few feet behind Mike Hardy's metal desk in the 1964th Communications Group building. The low, long, one-story building was quiet and deserted at this early hour. Mike took a sip of coffee and set aside the thick training manual he had come to catch up on, then pulled open his desk drawer and took out a different sort of manual—his Bible.

It was Mike's custom to arrive early for his daily quiet time, there at his desk with his back to the window as the morning light fell on the pages. Mike was new in his faith, and he felt he had so much to learn, so he began each morning storing away the protective power of the Scriptures to help guard and guide his heart and mind for the tasks of the day. He said a short prayer for himself and his family and opened his Bible to where he had left off reading the day before. As he read, the words seemed to jump off the page as the writer of the Psalms spoke confidently about physical protection promised to believers in times of danger.

In the past, Mike had viewed the Bible as a history book, full of old prophecies fulfilled thousands of years ago, but suddenly he sat up in his chair, paying attention. Currently there were tense anti-American sentiments in the vicinity. In the preceding months, several terrorist bombings had taken place at U.S. military bases in Germany, especially targeting communications buildings. Because of this, a concrete blast containment wall approximately six feet tall had been constructed all along the front of Mike's building, which was separated from the four-story headquarters building by a large parking lot.

Mike glanced at the window behind him. Even though the glass bricks stretched from floor to ceiling, it afforded no view. It was just as well, for the only view was of the parking lot. At present the lot was empty. By eight o'clock, however, hundreds of cars with American tags would fill it.

Mike slowly closed his Bible, mentally repeating a verse about God's protecting power, and then opened his training manual. Soon he was immersed in technical reading. He paused to turn the page and glanced down at his watch: 7:20 A.M.

Suddenly the manual leapt from the desk as a deafening explosion vibrated through Mike's ears. Everything in his office was creaking and shaking and moving—the desk, the ceiling, the floor. Mike's body vibrated like a roller coaster plunging down an uneven track. *A bomb's gone off in the hallway!* Mike thought as he held on to the desk as metal file cabinets came crashing down to the floor next to the doorway.

After the rattling stopped, Mike rubbed his eyes and coughed as the room filled up with a thick haze. *The building's on fire!* Mike thought. He jumped up from his desk and groped his way over toward the door, tripping over a ceiling tile. He looked up and saw that the acoustical tiles making up the suspended ceiling had been dislodged. *That's not smoke,* Mike realized. *That's dust coming down from the ceiling.*

Mike moved through the hallway door, crunching debris underfoot and groping his way to the front door. As he pushed through the door, he smelled gasoline burning.

The parking lot was unrecognizable. Across the lot, against the side of the headquarters building, was a pile of blackened metal car hulks thrown on top of each other as orange, angry flames shot up in an inferno as tall as the roof of the four-story building. *That explosion wasn't inside our building,* Mike realized. *It was a car bomb in the parking lot, and I was sitting right there with my back just a few feet from the window where it went off.*

"Evacuate the area!" someone yelled. Mike turned and escaped back through the communications building and out the back door. There he found more bizarre calling cards of the deadly force of the explosion. Large, charred chunks of metal from the car used in the blast had catapulted over the roof of the building and were littering the back lot. A single large coil from the car's suspension lay smoldering on the ground.

As sirens wailed, Mike began dusting the grit off his arms and face. Then he noticed something strange. Mike slid his hand down the back of his shirt. Not a rip or a tear. *You would have thought some of that glass from that window behind me would have at least torn my shirt,* he thought. *My window was right in line with that blast. I'm lucky I wasn't killed by shattering glass.*

Later that afternoon when Mike returned to his office, he surveyed the side of the block-long headquarters building facing the blast. Every single window on all four stories had been blown out by the tremendous force of the explosion. Then he turned to survey the communications building. In spite of the containment wall, every window had been shattered there, too, except for one lone window. That particular window was directly in front of the explosion, the only window where someone had been sitting at that early hour. That single unshattered window was the one in Mike's office, where he had been seated at 7:20 A.M. with his back just three feet away.

"I couldn't believe it," Mike said. "I went over and looked at that ordinary stack of glass bricks, wondering why it had survived the blast. All around the frame of the window were serious cracks, showing that a mighty force had indeed slammed against it. As I stood staring at the deep cracks in the wall around the windows, suddenly I remembered a Bible verse, 'The angel of the LORD encamps around those who fear him, and he delivers them' (Ps. 34:7). I pictured two strong heavenly beings standing there holding the window in place with their hands, their wings spread wide, and there was no doubt in my mind whatsoever that this was precisely what happened."

Mike finished his story. "If the bomb had gone off any later, the parking lot would have been full of people. Several people suffered cuts and bruises, and one man had a broken arm, but there were no serious injuries. But the most unbelievable part was what investigators found when they examined a big round hole that looked like a cannonball had been shot through the concrete wall of the headquarters building. Inside the building they discovered a metal canister. The canister was full of plastic explosives. Apparently two bombs had been planted, and for some reason, only the smaller one detonated. How that second, larger bomb could have hit that building with enough force to make a hole in the concrete without detonating the explosives packed inside is a total mystery. It was truly a miracle, because that second bomb would have completely demolished the entire headquarters building. I guess God's protecting angels were really busy there that day."

Mike's story is one of those inexplicable, mysterious happenings where prayer and Scripture worked together to display an unseen protective power that we do not fully understand. Mike prayed for protection, and he was sent a promise in Scripture that later proved literally true in a moment of ultimate peril.

But there are other days when the protecting power of the Scriptures answer our prayers for emotional support and help. How often do we feel alone, fearful, weak, doubting? Chancing upon the answering Scripture just as surely shatterproofs our inner lives, protecting us from falling into a million pieces (1 Cor. 10:13). Perhaps we will be given a verse to cling to that gives us unbreakable courage, unending love, or unbending trust. While we are looking for resolution, God instead gives us ironclad resolve. Scriptures are among the strongest of prayer answers. After all, Jesus says, "The Scripture cannot be broken" (John 10:35).

The Case of the Missing Keys

That hot July day our household was already thoroughly disorganized following an overnight camping trip. Gordon was sweeping pine straw off of the collapsed tent in the garage, blackened pots soaked in the sink, and the boys, then age five and three and quite cranky from lack of sleep, were leaving a trail of abandoned toys all over the den floor. Unfortunately, we had chosen this inopportune time to run an ad in the newspaper to sell Gordon's car, and the phone and doorbell were driving us crazy.

About two o'clock in the afternoon, when Gordon went to get his car keys to run downtown, the keys were not in their usual spot on the kitchen desk. Gordon tried to mentally retrace his steps since last seeing them: "I remember the lady test-driving my car and coming back up the driveway and handing me the keys. After that I swept the garage and went upstairs and changed clothes."

Based on his recollections of where he had been and what he had done, we looked in all of the likely places—the pocket of his jeans in the laundry basket, the garage, the car ignition, and the trunk lock. Nothing. Then we began looking in unlikely and totally bizarre places in the rooms where he had been—in the garbage can, in the bathtub, in the refrigerator, on the kitchen window ledges. Nothing.

Finally we gave up, hoping the keys would eventually turn up. Gordon borrowed my keys and took five-year-old Jeff with him on his errand downtown in the family station wagon. Half an hour later, Gordon telephoned home. "The station wagon just broke down on the interstate. We had to hike along the shoulder to the nearest exit, and Jeff was scared someone bad would stop and pick us up. Can you come and get us?"

"I can't," I stammered. "Your car's here, but no keys. We never found them."

"Oh, yeah," Gordon said, his voice trailing off.

I hung up the phone and jumped into emergency mode. *I've got to find those keys!* I thought. I hurried down the driveway and scoured the concrete with my eyes on the way back up. Finally I let loose of a small prayer, "Lord, I really need to find those keys."

As I was going back into the garage, I noticed the broom propped up in the corner. Suddenly a Bible verse jumped into my mind, and I repeated a paraphrase of it to myself: "The kingdom of God is like a woman [me] who has gold coins [two sets of car keys] and loses one. She lights a lamp, sweeps the house and searches diligently until she finds it. Then she calls her neighbors and rejoices" (Luke 15:8–9).

As I repeated the Scripture again, I seemed especially impressed with the words about sweeping since Gordon had been sweeping earlier that day. The thought came, *Maybe I should take this verse literally.* I raced to the broom closet. No luck. As I was standing in the kitchen, I happened to glance into the den. Something nagged in the back of my mind. *The toys,* I suddenly realized. *They've been picked up. Gordon must have done it on his way upstairs earlier and forgotten all about it. Since he didn't remember going in there, we never looked there. Could picking the toys up off the den floor be the* sweeping *that's been impressed on my mind?*

I rushed over to the toy cabinet and searched inside. Nothing but toys. I felt across the mantel with my hands. Nothing. I ran my hands along the top bookshelf. My hand bumped against a pile of cold metal. The car keys! Apparently Gordon had walked into the den with the keys in his hand, absent-mindedly put them up on the top shelf for safekeeping, and then tidied up the toys.

I put the keys in my pocket and gave them a little pat, a smile of merry irony spreading over my face at the strange verse that had directed me to look in the den. You see, in the Bible's version, the sweeping leads to finding. In our mixed-up version of the story that Saturday, it had been the sweeping that led to the losing. In some way only God could have orchestrated, the word *sweeping* had been just the clue I had needed, even though my "clue" had been written thousands of miles away and two thousand years earlier.

Scriptures often become surprising answers to prayer because they pack so many different applications into so few words. Scriptures can at the same time be about ancient people, and about us, and about Jesus and God, and about an imaginary character in a parable. They can have literal meanings and figurative meanings and prophetic meanings and historical meanings. None of these meanings are more particularly right than the others until they suddenly become quite practically useful depending on our current needs.

As I learned that July afternoon, we do not have time for Bible lessons when station wagons are broken down on the interstate and car keys are misplaced somewhere within half an acre of house and driveway. If we are serious about receiving prayer answers, we need to have a serious knowledge about what is available in the answer book. Once we have read, studied, and daily exposed ourselves to the Scriptures, the Holy Spirit is ready to help us succeed in the game of hide-and-seek that we often play with car keys and the keys to living available in the Bible (John 14:26).

Standing on the Promises

Aspiring musician Tricia Pilkington, of Clyde, North Carolina, took out her wallet and carefully counted out the money she had to cover her expenses at a three-day convention where she was to sing. "One, two, three," Tricia counted. She stopped and stared in dismay. That was all she had—three one-dollar bills to cover her food and gas. Tricia sighed and tucked the bills back into her wallet and sat down to pray. "Lord," she said, "you know I just spent a hundred and ninety dollars on tapes to sell at the convention, and I've got an appointment for a two-hundred-dollar recording session when I get back. I'm so thankful for the friend who's paying for my hotel room, but three dollars isn't going to stretch far enough to cover everything else. I guess I'm going to have to find some way to remember that I'm depending on you to get me there and back."

As soon as she had prayed, an idea came to Tricia. She got out a piece of paper and cut a small strip. Then she wrote on it, "The LORD will provide for all of your needs" (Gen. 22:14). Then she took off her shoe and put the paper in the insole and slipped her foot back in. "Well, God," she said, "I'm going to be literally and figuratively standing on your promises all weekend."

211

Just as Tricia was about to pull out of her driveway with that Bible verse tucked in her shoe, a neighbor appeared with a basket of food. "For your trip," she said. Tricia thanked her neighbor, and then she thanked God: "Thank you, Lord. I won't go hungry today because I've got a sandwich and a soda and some cucumbers. And especially thanks for the cucumbers. You know how much I love them."

When Tricia arrived at the convention hall carrying her guitar case, she straightened her shoulders and stood tall in her shoes, reminding herself, "God will provide." Then something odd happened. A woman came up to Tricia and handed her a five-dollar bill, saying, "God told me to give you this." Startled, Tricia studied the woman's face to see if she had met her before. No. She was a total stranger. Tricia thanked the woman profusely and tucked the bill into her purse. About fifteen minutes later, the scene repeated itself not once but twice, when two other women came forward with five dollars, each offering the same odd explanation. *You're so good, God,* Tricia thought. *You've already multiplied my money five times over.*

The spontaneous donations kept up all day. Most conventioneers slipped Tricia a five, but Tricia's heart was most touched by two hot, crumpled dollars carefully put into her hand by an elderly lady. As Tricia lost count of the growing cash in her purse, she became engaged in a conversation with a hurting woman, and in a moment of self-forgetfulness, she gave the woman ten dollars' worth of tapes. A friend noticed and said, "It will come back to you twofold." Sure enough, while the friend was still standing there, two women came up and each handed Tricia a ten-dollar bill.

When lunchtime came, someone insisted on paying for a hot lunch for Tricia. Another bought dinner for her at a waffle restaurant. Someone even offered, "Before you leave this weekend, I want to fill your car up with gas, oil, anything it needs."

By that evening, Tricia had amassed ninety-five dollars, received one woman at a time in an unusual and spontaneous outpouring of personal donations from conventioneers from all over the state, who, as far as Tricia knew, had not been alerted to her dire need by anyone except God. When Tricia's turn came to perform a song she had written, she received a standing ovation. Afterward, she sold $350 worth of tapes, enough to cover the costs of the tapes with enough left over to nearly cover her scheduled recording session.

That evening as Tricia was taking off her shoe in her hotel room, the paper with the Scripture written on it fell onto the floor. One of her roommates saw it and asked, "What in the world is that thing? Why have you been walking around all day with a piece of paper in your shoe?"

Tricia picked up the limp piece of paper and said, "I put it there to remind me that I'm standing on God's promise that he'll provide for me."

When Tricia arrived back home she laughed as she told me, "That paper looked pretty ratty after three days in my shoe, but I saved it to help me remember how God provided for me."

Although we may not be struggling artists like Tricia, we all struggle when it comes to consistently applying scriptural promises as answers to prayer. Of course, Scriptures are not magic charms. We should not unnecessarily place ourselves in foolish situations, expecting God to bend the rules of the universe to rescue us (Luke 4:12). But the majority of us do not need words of caution. We usually need a rattling call to courage to take God at his word.

People have been trusting God's promises since the dawn of history. Standing on God's promises, of course, is not literally about legs and feet. To stand means to maintain one's position, to be firm and steadfast. When we "stand on" something, it means that we are depending upon it.

After Moses told of God's coming blessings in the promised land, he told the people, "Fix these words of mine in your hearts and minds" (Deuteronomy 11:18). Often we pray Scriptures thinking we are reminding God of his promises, when we are really the ones the prayer is helping to change. Trusting God's promises does not bring resolution, but rather brings resolve. Our prayers are answered by giving us sustaining power. They help us hang on and get through, encouraging us with the hope that as we take difficult steps of faith, God will provide the supporting help. Just as Tricia put a piece of paper in her shoe to make up for what was lacking in her wallet, so we, too, might overcome our lack of courage by filling up our minds with God's words that where he leads, He will provide.

Curtain Call across the South China Sea

Early one fall morning in 1985, seventy-one-year-old Helen Lane, the step-grandmother of Lucy Lane Corwin from chapter 2, was asleep and dreaming when a voice spoke three words to her in her small retirement apartment in her North Palm Beach high-rise. The voice said, "Enlarge your tents." Helen was so startled that she woke right up. "Lord," she said, "what on earth does that mean? I live in a modern high-rise, not a tent."

Helen loves a good mystery, so she fixed a cup of coffee and chatted over the strange message with the Lord. "Dear Lord, I'm a widow and I'm old. I'm certainly not expecting to raise any more children. If anything, at my age you downsize, you don't enlarge." But the thought came back as clearly as the sun rising over the brink of the Atlantic beyond her apartment balcony. "Enlarge your tent."

All morning Helen prayed, "Show me what this means." Around midmorning, it came to her that the words might be from the Bible. After searching through the concordance, she turned to Isaiah 54:2 (KJV): "Enlarge the place of thy tent, and let them stretch forth the curtains of thine habitations: spare not, lengthen thy cords and strengthen thy stakes."

Helen closed up her Bible, still quite puzzled. Nothing more came to her. Over the course of the next month, she often opened her Bible to that verse, wondering what those words might mean. Then in December, a larger apartment on the twelfth floor with a nice guest bedroom and a second bath came on the market. *It's a marvelous buy,* Helen thought. *I'll take it.* She bought it, moved in, and set up a bed in her new, empty guest room, waiting to see who God would send to occupy it.

Several months later, Helen chanced to meet an acquaintance named Peter at a fellowship meeting. Peter pulled her aside. "Mrs. Lane, I have a story to tell you. I'm in the merchant marines, and on December 13, we were sailing the South China Sea when we encountered sixty-four Vietnamese boat people adrift in a tiny boat. We took them aboard and learned that they had been at sea for five days with no food and only a few sips of water. At five o'clock the next morning I was astonished when one of them, a young woman of about eighteen, came to the galley and began helping make breakfast. Through a translator, I learned that her name was Haun and that she had been praying to escape Communism for many years. By the time we got to the detainment camp in the Philippines, Haun had earned the respect of the entire crew because of her resourcefulness and her faith. When we parted, I vowed that I would try and help her."

Peter said, "Mrs. Lane, I believe that you have the means to help Haun. Her prayers will only be answered if someone sponsors her and takes her into their home. I promise she won't be a bit of trouble to you. She's kindhearted and so helpful."

Standing there in that meeting room, Peter's tale so impressed Helen that she could indeed picture this stranger named Haun coming to America to live with her and everything would be just fine. Could this be the meaning behind that mysterious Bible verse? Could this young girl, plucked from the sea on the other side of the world, be the one meant to occupy an empty bed in her new guest bedroom? *After all,* Helen thought, *she was rescued in December, and that's exactly when my new apartment became available.*

Helen patiently filed the massive immigration paperwork, eventually filling up a two-inch-thick file in the process. Nearly a year later, on January 5, 1987, a thin, dark-haired girl with lovely almond eyes came hesitantly through the gate at the Palm Beach airport. "Mom?" she murmured shyly when she saw Helen. Helen nodded and they both broke into grins.

"Dear, can I help you with your bags?" Helen asked pleasantly. Haun's mouth froze into a frown as she pinned uncomprehending eyes on Helen.

Dear Lord, Helen thought, *surely after a year in the refugee camp she's learned some English. How on earth are we going to live together if we can't communicate?*

Helen managed to get Haun up the elevator to her apartment using nods and gestures. The next morning at breakfast, the two tried to settle on where Haun should sit at the table. Haun wagged her head and sat at the place nearest the kitchen, not in the chair Helen pointed out. Haun looked at Helen with a furrowed forehead, her lips imparting strange syllables, presumably in explanation.

"That's fine," Helen nodded, feeling her stomach tighten as she thought, *I didn't understand a word of that. Where to sit at a table is such a little thing. What will we do about the important things you just can't get across with gestures?*

Before the week was finished, Helen enrolled Haun in a special high school program for immigrants. Then she prayed, "Honest to goodness, Lord, help her to catch on to English quickly. We can't live like this."

Haun expressed with the perpetual motion of a cleaning cloth the things she was unable to say in words. Helen often found her out on the balcony, vigorously washing the sliding glass door. Haun shook her head suspiciously over the dishwasher and then washed all of the plates by hand. Finally it dawned on Helen that Haun had chosen the seat at the table nearest the kitchen door for convenience in serving meals. Her actions spoke clearly, "I want to make myself a useful person and make you glad that I am here."

You are a useful person, and I'm so glad you're here, dear, Helen wanted to sing back. She could only shake her head, thinking, *Peter was right. Haun hasn't given me a moment's trouble, other than this ache deep down in my heart about this language barrier.*

After two weeks, Helen laid her hands on an English/Vietnamese dictionary. Finally the two could distinguish one word at a time, such as bread and cake. Six months passed, and the two made little progress beyond sign language. Helen realized that her prayer that Haun quickly catch on to English was not destined to be answered.

One day as Helen was driving down I-95 to pick up Haun at a gas station where she was dropped off after school, Helen began to think over their difficult living situation. Helen had always been a great communicator, having successfully built careers in radio and public relations in the days before such doors were fully opened for women. As she drove, Helen poured out her heart to God. "I really don't mind that I'm seventy and she's twenty. I understand and

217

respect our different cultures and upbringings, and even our different denominations. But this language barrier is the biggest challenge of my whole life. I'm too old for this. My heart is breaking for Haun, and I'm just as frustrated as I can be. Enlarging my tent is one thing, but stretching it out until it falls apart is another. Did I misunderstand what you were trying to say to me?"

Helen's fretting was abruptly interrupted when the steering wheel froze up right under her hands. *Oh, no, the power steering's gone out,* Helen thought as she jammed on the brakes. The brake pedal did not give. *Now the brakes are locked,* Helen thought in a panic. "Lord, help me," Helen cried out as her hands helplessly gripped the steering wheel of the runaway car as trucks and cars whizzed by. Suddenly a thought jumped into her mind: *Put the car into neutral.* Helen threw the gearshift, tugged with all of her might on the steering wheel, and the car finally halted in a flurry of gravel on the shoulder.

Now what do I do, Lord? Helen wondered shakily as she got out of the car and stood trying to calm herself by the side of the interstate.

At that instant a woman pulled over and asked, "Are you having trouble?"

"More trouble than you can imagine," Helen replied. "I've got a little Vietnamese girl waiting for me at a gas station who doesn't speak a word of English, and my car is completely broken down."

"Get in," the woman said. "We'll go and pick her up, then I'll take you both home."

As the woman drove, Helen found herself pouring out the whole story about Haun and how she could speak only a word or two of English.

The woman said, "I know a Vietnamese priest at a church that isn't far from where you live. I'm sure if you go and talk to him, he can help." The woman scribbled down the priest's name. Helen stared down at the paper. *This is too many coincidences for one day,* she thought. *First my car breaks down just as a woman's driving by who knows a Vietnamese priest, and then the priest's name turns out to be Father Peter, just like my friend Peter in the merchant marines who first met Haun.*

As soon as her car was running again, Helen took Haun over to meet Father Peter. Helen was relieved to discover that Father Peter spoke perfect English with a charming British accent. Helen and Haun sat down, and words began flying from their mouths at the same time. After about ten minutes of this Vietnamese-English barrage, the priest asked, "Mrs. Lane, how long did you stay in Vietnam?"

"I've never been there," Helen stammered.

He wrinkled his forehead, "This is very strange. Haun is speaking to me in Vietnamese, and you are speaking to me in English, yet you are both talking about the same subject at the same time. In fact, sometimes you seem to know what Haun is thinking before she says it."

Helen sat back in astonishment as Father Peter repeated his remarks in Vietnamese to Haun. A smile lit up Haun's face, and then both women laughed at the same moment. Helen thought, *Well, Lord, I do love a good mystery, and this is one of them. I thought following your directions had stretched me out too far, but now I see that where my ability ends, your power begins. It's up to us to answer the call and after that trust you to provide.*

The two went back home, still using a few broken phrases between them and still stuck with the cumbersome process of looking up words in the dictionary to get across their thoughts and ideas. But this time Helen no longer felt hopeless and helpless, for she was relying on God to fill in the gaps.

Eventually Haun married and had two children. Then one Christmas, she presented a very special gift to Helen. It was a bamboo curtain, the kind meant to be hung across a doorway. Haun said, "You take me from behind Bamboo Curtain. I shall never forget your kindness when you get me."

"What a lovely gift," Helen said, thinking back to the verse that had instructed her to "stretch forth the curtains of thine habitation." *Never in my wildest imaginations, Lord,* she thought with a laugh, *did I imagine you were talking about a bamboo curtain.*

Just as Helen's inability to understand everything that Haun was thinking and feeling made her begin to question the value of their whole relationship, we are often discouraged by the huge gaps in our understanding of the Bible. At times we wonder if we will ever get past the strange customs, the odd phrasing, the symbolism, and the footnotes. And when we finally find a sensible general principle we can grasp, we are perplexed by its brevity.

Often we tire of the seeming vagueness of Scripture. We wish that God would give us a complete computer printout with our names clearly printed at the top, telling us specifically what we should do. Instead, he says magnificently and mysteriously, "Stretch forth." All at once we are tantalized by the click and clatter of a bamboo curtain being moved by a slight breeze, and we begin imagining faraway lands, and distant people, and the corners of the world that we have yet to see. We finally understand that God has put a holy thirst inside of the human soul for discovery. We do not want to be told what life is all about; we want to experience it, and explore it, and feel the wonder when the puzzle pieces finally fit together as we see a stunning picture emerge from the disorganized fragments. For it is this prospect of discovery that keeps our faith vital and our hearts forever young.

Jesus says, "The kingdom of heaven is like treasure hidden in a field. When a man found it, he hid it again, and then in his joy went and sold all he had and bought that field" (Matt. 13:44). Without the search, the joy of finding is diminished. Curiosity is the best friend of faith, and the first step in a lifetime of finding. This in itself is our treasure, our gift, when we question and search until we finally find. And that is why God always loves a good mystery.

Living Out the Scriptures

In a day of round-the-clock news channels and instant e-mail, the final wonder is how such incredibly old news as the Scriptures could be anything more than ancient, fossil-ized compost. After all, the most recent events reported in the Bible are perhaps two thousand years old by now, and the very oldest event—the creation of the universe—stretches back to the beginning of time. Yet the Bible continues to speak to us in our time, day after day, week after week, in living rooms, bedrooms, Sunday school rooms, and hospi-tal rooms all around the world. How could our needs be so directly met, our burning questions be so ably addressed by ancient writers who never imagined the complexities of modern life as they rolled pieces of parchment and sealed them in clay jars in goatskin tents?

As we pray, God may send an answer to us using words he spoke eons ago. As people all over the world bow their heads in prayer, God mysteriously "rewrites" Scripture daily and hourly without changing so much as a dash or a period, for he is writing not on paper but on a new and unlikely medium. For as an astonishing way of answering our prayers, God declares, "I will put my laws in their minds, and write them on their hearts" (Heb. 8:10). And so let us open our Bibles and our hearts, waiting for God's answers.

8

SURPRISED
BY POWER

Pray continually.

1 Thessalonians 5:17

When I unfolded the newspaper that October morning, my heart did a flip-flop. There on the front page was a picture of Dick, husband of my friend Deanna, with a big black headline reading, "Asked to Resign by City Officials." I sped to Dick and Deanna's house, my mind jumbled up with worry. *Dick works in a specialized government field, and there aren't any more jobs for him in this whole area. They'll have to move, they'll have to sell their house, Deanna will lose her customer*

223

base for her home-sales business, the children will have to be
yanked out of school.

While Deanna unlatched the screen door, the phone was
ringing. As soon as I stepped into the kitchen, Deanna's four-
year-old daughter proceeded to knock a glass brimming with
orange juice all over the floor. Deanna and I both fell to our
knees, frantically applying paper towels in jerky movements
like we were killing yellow jackets.

Deanna could not even speak in sentences. "That phone.
Everybody wants to know what happened. But we don't even
know. Politics! The kids! They're driving me crazy."

I had come over thinking I would pray with Deanna,
but how on earth do you pray calmly when all sense of
organization has flown out the window with the morning
headlines?

When we had done our best cleaning up the juice spill, I
suggested, "Have you got a couple of pieces of paper?"

Deanna rummaged through a drawer and came up with
some notebook paper. We sank down onto the living-room
sofa where the drapes were tightly drawn. "I sort through things
better on paper," I explained. "Let's write a prayer plan."

Deanna seemed surprised. "I thought prayer was something you just did. I've never heard of planning it."

To be honest, I had not tried it before either, but it was
all I could think of at the moment. "As an experiment, let's
make a prayer worksheet. What do you want to see happen
out of this situation?"

As we talked it through, the idea began to make more
sense. We roughed in three main categories. The first was
the overall, lifetime future that God could work out through
this unfortunate event, that he would be glorified somehow
and that Dick and Deanna would someday be able to help
others going through a job loss. Next we thought through
what was needed for the resolution concerning a new job

for Dick. Here we listed specific ideas: that it be somewhere near the West Coast where their family lived, that it would be a good environment for the girls, that they would find a good church where they could grow and learn. Lastly, we listed things necessary for the immediate future while Dick was in the process of looking for a new job, such as patience, forgiveness, and daily help to see to all of the details of selling the house and moving.

We prayed the list through that morning, then ended with an agreement to pray individually over the list, one point at a time as we felt appropriate. As Deanna posted her list on her refrigerator, she said, "It's so strange. I know I should be falling apart, but I feel so calm."

Her words both excited and troubled me. What if this experiment did not work?

In the next few months, there were plenty of stressful circumstances for Dick and Deanna. There was Christmas without a paycheck, expenses for plane fares to job interviews that did not turn up an offer, fix-up jobs to market the house. Worst of all was the uncertainty. At those times, the prayer sheet turned out to be a helpful counterbalance to Deanna's emotions. Many times when she was tired, stressed out, impatient, or fearful, she could look at her prayers there in black and white, never rising and falling with her emotional highs and lows. Soon Deanna was sharing openly with whomever offered a worried word of sympathy that she was trusting in God's help.

On March 18, five months after we made our prayer list, Deanna phoned me with the news that Dick had been offered a job in Arizona. The city just happened to be where Dick's uncle and one of Deanna's business connections lived. Deanna was overcome with excitement.

I thanked God, folded up our prayer sheet, and stuck it in my journal, relieved that the experiment had worked and that our prayers about Dick's new job had been answered as meticulously as someone checking off each point with a razor-sharp pencil.

Dick and Deanna soon moved away. In the intervening years, I moved three times myself. Eventually we lost touch. Then twelve years later, I answered the phone and heard a perky voice on the other end. "Hi, this is Deanna, remember me?"

Deanna explained that she was visiting friends in a neighboring suburb and had managed to find me in the phone directory. As we chatted, she went on to share twelve years' worth of good news—that Dick was now working with a charitable foundation, that they loved living in Arizona, that they had found a fabulous church right away, and that the girls were now grown up and college-bound. Then she said something that amazed me. "You don't know how many times over the years I've thought about you and wanted to call you or write you to tell you how much that prayer list has meant in my life."

After we said good-bye, I wondered, *How could a prayer list that was all finished up and the answers checked off twelve years ago still be impacting Deanna's life?* Intrigued, I dug through my journals to figure out the reason. As I looked over the list, I saw that for one thing, the list had not just asked for material things like jobs and houses but had also asked for graces like patience and forgiveness and God's glory. Was that the reason it had been so effective? Was that the reason Deanna still thought about it with gratitude?

As I sat there with my journal open, God dropped a new understanding into my mind. "Karen," he seemed to tell me, "there wasn't a magic formula in what you prayed. It's not so much what you say or what you ask. What counts is that you are praying. Deanna learned to trust me enough to ask for what she needed. Learning that is something that lasts long after the situations you are praying about are resolved and forgotten. In fact, the trust you learn when you bring your daily needs to me lasts forever."

Special Delivery at the Mailbox

As we conclude our investigation of prayer answers, we are poised to have our lives forever changed just like Deanna. Are we ready to get serious about seeing prayer answers in our lives? If so, the first step is to begin asking. This sounds so simple that it seems to go without saying, but as we have seen throughout these pages, it is often the most obvious things that escape us. There must come a moment when we transform petition from a routine "give us this day our daily bread" briefly mouthed at the dinner table into a working reality in our lives.

My friend Charlene, whom we met in the rock-fish story in chapter 1, remembers the exact moment and place it happened to her: at the bottom of her steep New Jersey driveway one winter morning. That particular day, several inches of snow had fallen. Charlene buckled her two preschool children into the car for a trip to the doctor's and aimed her car straight down the driveway toward the road.

Charlene said, "As I started down the driveway, I felt the car begin to slide. I realized I had no control. The car slid off the driveway and right into the mailbox. I had been going slow enough that there wasn't any damage to the car or the mailbox, but I knew I was stuck. I thought, *I'm late for the doctor's, and I've got to get out right away. But how? I'll never be able to get enough traction to back the car up the hill.* Unfortunately, all of my neighbors worked during the day, and there was no one nearby I could call on to push me out.

"As I sat there trying to figure out what to do, the thought came into my mind, *Maybe I should pray about it.* An answering thought came back, *Do you really think it will do any good?*

"Finally I gave in to the urge to pray. 'God,' I prayed, 'please help me get out.' Then I put the car in reverse. The wheels made a grinding sound, and the next instant I backed up onto the driveway as if it were completely clear and dry. I pulled out onto the street and went on my way with a really incredulous feeling. I thought, *Oh, my goodness, something actually happened right after I prayed. God must have answered.*"

Petition as the Doorway to Faith

Charlene's story intrigued me because, like Deanna's twelve-year-old prayer sheet, Charlene was still talking about her mailbox prayer over lunch twenty years after it happened. All those years later and there she sat, telling me how she had been a grown woman with two children to raise, not knowing that she herself was the one needing to begin a growth spurt. How long had God been literally and figuratively waiting at the mailbox for Charlene to post him a prayer that he could answer? Until Charlene deliberately decided to take the plunge on that specific plea for God's help, no possibilities of answered prayer existed in her life. Without that experimental prayer, Charlene would have pulled out onto the road that long-ago winter morning, believing in friction, traction, and tire treads. Instead, she left with a flutter in her stomach about the gigantic possibilities of a daily relationship with a God as close as the letterbox, and her life took a completely new direction.

Based on the ease with which children ask God for such outlandish things as baby brothers and sisters and then just as easily ask God after a few months to please take the baby back, we conclude that asking God for the things that we want and need is an inborn trait. Adults, on the other hand, do not naturally ask. The act of petitioning God is at odds with the self-reliant independence of adulthood. In the same way that we are born to prayer as children and raise ourselves on skepticism as we mature, we must go through a second coming-of-age if we are to receive answers to prayer. Although it may seem that we are becoming childlike when we again dare to ask God for things, there is nothing child-like in the fierce battle that goes on within our minds as we wrestle with ourselves over whether or not to ask.

We often put off our second coming-of-age until a dire emergency, when praying is our only hope. On the other hand, our final coming-of-age might start with a sigh of frustration over some daily dilemma that plunges us into uncertainty. Will praying really do any good? Is this too small and trivial a thing to be bothering God about?

We teeter-totter up and down, yes and no, spending all of our time differentiating over the big and little things and none of our time petitioning over anything. Petition is hum-bling because it lays bare our needs and our utter poverty. Petition also highlights our undisciplined religious habits. We sit down to ask, suddenly realizing that we should have called upon God eons ago for other purposes, such as thank-ing him or praising him or confessing to him. And lastly, petition worries us. If God does in fact give us this favor, what will he expect in return?

The decision we now face after enjoying all of the delight-ful answers to prayer we have shared in this book is simply this: Will we again take up the habit of asking so that we might be set free to experience the surprising joy of receiv-ing? This happens only when we no longer treat petition as the bothersome stepchild of prayer, but rather as a holy avocation and the doorway to faith.

Daniel considered petition so vital that he was willing to put his life on the line for his right to bring his needs before

God. Most of us recall that Daniel was thrown into the lion's den, but few of us remember that he was thrown in for disobeying the king's edict that said, "Whosoever shall ask a petition of any God or man for thirty days, save of thee, O King, he shall be cast into the den of lions" (Dan. 6:7 KJV). Daniel committed his "crime" by continuing his custom of kneeling by his window, facing Jerusalem, to pray three times a day.

For Daniel, petition was not an optional part of prayer. Let thirty days go by without asking? Heavens, no! Daniel was unwilling to let even one-third of a day slip by without calling on God for help. I suppose it is no accident that Daniel survived for a whole night in a pit full of hungry lions, because Daniel and God were no strangers.

The closing chapter in our investigation is about turning us from recipients into witnesses, filled with unshakable power. It is about having an inventory brimming full of answered prayer. The time has come to develop our prayer-answer sensors, to see a flash of awe and joy go off in our souls when we realize that God has worked on our behalf. Are we ready to take the first step?

Life in Rocking-Horse Heaven

I parked the minivan on the street and walked down the concrete driveway that cuts along the side of the turn-of-the-century cottage with a deep front porch. There, behind the house, sat what used to be a wooden garage and what was now rocking-horse heaven.

John and Ann Sprankell greeted me, wearing jeans dusted with sawdust, and gave me a tour of their workshop. As I stood in the tiny cubbyhole where skeins of yarn are stapled onto the handcrafted wooden horses to make manes and tails, John told me about an answer to prayer that set us all to laughing.

It seems that one day in 1995, John received an answer from God about whether or not to launch full-time into the rocking-horse business in—of all places—a men's rest room in Ohio. There he found his answer, written on a piece of paper taped to the wall right above the gents' plumbing fixture.

After we finished laughing, John put the story into context by explaining that he had worked for twenty years as a factory supervisor in Jackson Center, Ohio, but his employment had been terminated when he was forty-four. After a year and a half of unemployment, the family found themselves eleven thousand dollars in debt. They migrated to Dayton, Tennessee, where John was hired on the second shift at a reclining-chair assembly plant.

As Christmas approached, their eight-year-old daughter, Shelley, came up with a mile-long list of all of the popular plastic toys. "I'm not wasting money on that junk," John told Ann. "I think I'll make her something out in the workshop that will last."

John ordered plans, but when Ann saw them, she was not enthusiastic. "Why a rocking horse? I thought you'd build her a nice toy chest or something."

Undaunted, John went about his stealthy work of making the rocking horse, and Ann painted on the finishing touches of purple frills and flowers. On Christmas morning, when John carried the rocking horse into the living room, Shelley leaped on the horse and after doing a few delirious rocks, she jumped off the horse and dove into John's lap, bawling, "Daddy, I can't believe you made it!"

From that moment, John was hooked. Word got around, and soon John gave up making wooden knickknacks to sell at craft shows and was turning out horses. John thought, *Haven't I been praying for a way to get out of debt? I'll never be able to do it on my salary from the factory. Could it be that the Lord sent us this rocking-horse idea?*

One day when the couple was packing up the van to go to a craft show, Ann said, "We've got to have a name for this business."

She came up with name after name and John kept shaking his head and saying, "Sorry, that name isn't it."

Finally Ann said, "I give up. I'm going to have a great big button made and I'm going to pin it on my shirt and it's going to have an arrow pointing to you that says, 'It's his idea.'"

"Sweetie," John said, "you just named the business. We'll call it 'His Idea Crafts' because it was God's idea in the first place."

In the fall of 1988, the couple was excited when they secured an order for twenty-five rocking horses from a major gift shop in Pigeon Forge, Tennessee. The only problem was that the twenty-five horses had yet to be built. The sawing, sanding, and assembling would have to be squeezed into the morning hours after John's factory shift. Despite the exhausting schedule, John felt wonderfully alive as he talked out loud to God in his workshop over the hum of the band saw.

As the years went by, the couple figured small ways to streamline the tedious handwork and upped production to thirty horses a week. After six years of hard work, John's prayer was answered when the eleven-thousand-dollar debt was paid off.

Then in 1995, John mentioned a subject that had been on his mind for some time. "Ann, I've been thinking. Should I go into the rocking-horse business full time? It seems awful risky, but sometimes after delivering rocking horses all weekend, I'm so tired when I drive those forty-five miles out to the factory, I don't even know how I got there."

"But if you quit, we'll lose our medical benefits," Ann pointed out. "And if the economy gets bad, are people going to be putting their money into rocking horses? We're not kids anymore. We'd have to get a real clear confirmation from the Lord to do something that crazy."

"You're right," John said. "It's a really scary step."

Soon afterward, the couple was visiting back in Ohio when their daughter Shelley, now sixteen, told John, "Daddy, please don't go back to the factory when we get home. One of these days you're going to kill yourself falling asleep at the wheel. You can be a much better witness at home in your workshop than you can in the factory."

John straightened up and asked, "How do you figure that?"

"Everybody in town knows you," Shelley said. "They know that you're fifty-five, and if they see you going out on your own and trusting God, that's going to say more than any words you could possibly ever say."

Wow, John thought, *how'd she get so smart? But this is really a serious step. I'm sure not going to do it without some sort of rock-solid confirmation.* Suddenly, John thought of Pastor Pete, whose church they had occasionally visited over in neighboring Botkins, Ohio. "Lord," John prayed, "for some reason I feel like if I drive over there for the evening service tonight, something Pastor Pete says will be a message just for me, whether it's in the sermon or something he tells me when I talk to him afterward."

So with this serious decision weighing in the balance, John took off driving alone, sipping a soft drink to calm his nerves. When he arrived at the church, John detoured to the men's room, and as he stood there, his eyes wandered to a piece of paper on the wall. Someone had typed a few sentences on a piece of paper, cut it out with pinking sheers and taped it to the wall above the plumbing fixture. Intrigued, John read the words, "Have I not commanded you? Be strong and courageous, do not be terrified, do not be discouraged, for the LORD your God will be with you wherever you go" (Josh. 1:9).

John says, "Everybody gets a kick out of me finding that Scripture there on the bathroom wall. But as soon as I read it, I knew it was why I'd driven over there. In fact, I was so sure that the verse was for me that I never even talked to Pastor Pete.

"The next day when it was time to drive home, I started silently praying, 'God, give me peace about this.' Somewhere past Dayton, Ohio, I finally felt it. I threw my hand up in the air and said, 'Yes! No more chair factory! I'm not going back.'"

Ordinarily, I would have snapped off my tape recorder on the paint-splattered shelf and thanked John and Ann for their time. Then I would have gone home to write a story about a factory worker being led to make rocking horses and then being sent on a scavenger hunt to find a confirming message taped up in a men's rest room in a town hundreds of miles away from home. As we conclude our investigation, however, the whole point is to wonder what will happen next. The theme of this chapter is not just about answers, but about answering power. It is not about lives nicely fixed by prayer answers, but about lives so set on fire by prayer that the future is changed because we are changed. The question before us is this: What astounding things will happen if we continue?

And so as my tape recorder continued to whir on the narrow back porch where John perched on a low stool and Ann sat painting rocking-horse faces, I heard the rest of the remarkable story.

John explained, "I taped a copy of that Bible verse onto my band saw and over my bed. The most exciting thing is that each day here at the shop there's so much more opportunity to see God at work. When I worked in the factory, I didn't need to look for God because everything was so routine. You knew what was going to happen next, when the whistle was going to blow, when you were going to get your paycheck. Here you're on pins and needles. You walk into the shop wondering, 'What is God going to do today?'"

As an example, John told me how they had been afraid to raise the price on the horses, even though they only had a slim profit margin on each one. He prayed, and soon afterward a stranger from Chattanooga walked up John's driveway to pick up several horses for a relative. They got to talking, and John told him about his pricing dilemma. The fellow replied, "I've been in the furniture industry all of my life, and I've worked in marketing. I can tell you exactly what formula the furniture industry uses for pricing." John sat down and applied the formula and finally had the courage to raise the price. The horses kept selling. "See?" John told me. "The Lord brought the right person right to my door."

Then he went into another tale of provision. After a while it became apparent they were losing money on the wholesale business, but opening their own retail store in a small college town was impractical. John again asked the Lord for specific direction. At a local business conference John bumped into someone who suggested, "Why not sell your rocking horses on the Internet?"

"The Internet?" John answered. "I don't know a thing about it. We don't even own a computer, and I can't afford to run out and buy one."

"I'll loan you a computer, and you can take a few months to see what's on the Web," the man replied.

After looking over the Internet, John decided that a web site was the way to go, but of course he could not afford to hire an expert to develop one. John prayed again, and a friend who liked to fiddle with computers volunteered to help. The next thing he knew, John had a web site up and running called "allhishorses.com," for the grand total of $119.

As I listened, it all began to blend together, answer after answer—a random meeting in a coffee shop with a business professor whose three students picked John as a project to upgrade the web site, and another man who wandered up the driveway and told John about a specialty photographer who lived up on the mountain and who eventually produced top-quality shots for the web site that showed the lovely details of Ann's painting on the horses. Listening to John, it nearly seemed that all it took to run a mom-and-pop business on a shoestring budget was prayer—and a driveway that God could send the right person wandering down.

John topped all of these stories with the van story. One day last summer, two major checks failed to arrive, and the workshop fell silent because there was no money for wood. They had been driving a decrepit van that had tight manual steering and brakes that were difficult for Ann to operate. Just as the shop shut down, the van broke down, and the mechanic across the street delivered the bad news that the van was beyond repair.

John says, "I walked down the driveway talking right out loud to God the same way I always do. I said, 'Lord, you know I need a van to make big deliveries. This is your business, and you know where my new van is sitting right now. I only ask for three things: power steering, power brakes, and air conditioning.'"

John walked off the driveway and sat down on the swing on the back porch. "I sat there all afternoon, never turning a lick, just talking to the Lord and swinging and dozing. I did the same thing the whole next day, just sitting there in peace, believing that God was taking care of it."

John finished, "Seven weeks later, I paid fifteen hundred cash for that white van sitting out there. Business just took an upturn, those checks came in, and Jimmy across the street called me and said he had a van out back that belonged to a fellow who had to go into a nursing home and would I like to buy it? The first time I drove that van down the road I said, 'God, you're awesome. This van's got everything I asked for, but you also threw in a tilt wheel, and cruise control, and electric windows, and door locks, too!'"

John summed up by saying, "If we had a big bankroll, we wouldn't be depending on God anymore. If we had a brand-new van, we'd forget to stop and pray about getting to where we're going. The way I see it, we're already rich. I'm paying my bills, and I'm working out here at my own pace, and every time I walk out my back door and walk into my little shop, I'm wondering what God will do next. I'm the luckiest guy in the whole world."

As I turned off my tape recorder, thinking that at last I had captured the whole story, John added the final exclamation point. "Yes indeed. It's amazing the people that God sends walking down the driveway," John said. "When Ann came home and told me that she'd met you at that meeting today and you might be dropping by, I knew right away it was another answer to prayer because I've been wanting someone to write this story for three years."

I gave a startled glance over at the ordinary concrete driveway that I had walked down an hour earlier, suddenly realizing that without knowing it, I, too, had been strangely led by God right to the Sprankells' workshop door even though it was not marked by so much as a sign. I had driven 150 miles to a town I had never set foot in, to speak at a small women's meeting. At the end of the meeting, I had simply held the door open for Ann Sprankell, who mentioned in passing that she had to get back to work painting rocking horses.

I nodded, thinking, *And I thought I was following my nose for a good story when I parked my van out front and walked down that driveway. But I was wrong. I'm another in a long line of people who happened to take that short walk without having any earthly idea that they had been drawn here by the great God of prayer.*

As I said good-bye to Ann and John, I was reluctant to leave rocking-horse heaven. Interestingly enough, the wonderful rocking horses were only the window dressing. For the true heaven housed in that dusty workshop was the daily dependence on a God who hears and answers our prayers.

Transformed by One Hundred Answers to Prayer

On the morning of January 22, I had no idea I was about to discover the heaven housed in my own small part of the world. It all started when I noticed a family's name in a routine listing of new members on the back of our church bulletin. As soon as I saw their address, I drew a big circle around it because it was an answer to a yearlong prayer.

Every weekday morning as I walk a two-mile loop around our neighborhood, I pray over the homes I pass. Our neighborhood is still under construction, with new homes being built and people constantly moving in and out. Since I did not know those on the other side of the subdivision, I took to offering general prayers for the occupants of the homes, usually praying over new houses, "Help them find a church where they can learn about you and grow and serve."

Every weekday it was the same pattern: walk, pray, walk, pray. Nothing remarkable happened. No strangers burst out of a freshly painted house and asked me, "Do you know of any good churches? Lately I've been feeling the need for God in my life." Walk, pray, spring, summer, autumn, winter. Then on January 22, there was a family listed on the back of the church bulletin with an address right on the road I prayed over daily.

As I started to put the bulletin on a journal page to commemorate this answered prayer, I noticed under previous church affiliation this notation: "profession of faith." *What?* I thought, *This family hasn't just transferred from another nice church in another city, they've walked straight from no church into our church. This couple is making a first-time commitment to God and his work!*

By now my heart was pumping just as vigorously as it does on my morning walks. In a reckless moment of exuberance I scribbled in my journal, "Since I'm writing a book on prayer answers, why not do an experiment where I try and note in my journal one hundred answers to prayer? I'll begin by counting this as number one."

Immediately my good sense took over. One hundred answers! Was that even possible? *Maybe I should just try for ten days or ten answers,* I thought. *Surely that will be good enough.*

An answering thought came back, *One hundred answers. It has to be one hundred because it sounds so impossible, so remarkable, so ridiculous, so unattainable.*

I finally let myself declare, "Well, I'm going to try it." I decided to organize it by categorizing the answers into the types of prayer answers we have encountered in this book: action, presence, word, call to pray, partnership, Scripture. As a final thought, I decided to record the approximate length of time between when I first prayed the request and when the answer had come. I was all set. Now all I needed were ninety-nine more prayer answers.

On the first day, I was quite pleased when I wrote down three answers to prayer. On the second day, however, instead of a prayer answer, I found myself writing, "I'm thinking hard, trying to see an answer today. I have a dull way of praying the same thing over and over, such as 'be with' Gordon at work. I had no idea my prayer life was in such a rut and so unfocused. I'll have to pray more specifically." And so I got to work, praying a bit more specifically concerning the long hours Gordon was putting in on an overwhelming work assignment.

That night when Gordon came home he asked, "What did you pray for me today?"

Since he had never asked such a thing before, I had a hard time remembering. Finally I said, "That you'd have the strength to get through."

"Anything else?"

"And that you'd get the help you need."

"Aha!" he said. "Today I got two new people who will really be great. They've got the skills and experience, and they're both available right away. I've already put together a new organizational plan of how to delegate responsibilities."

Our whole conversation was written in my journal as answer to prayer number four; the category was action, because it had been a turn of events connected to something I had prayed.

After that, I began praying more specifically and began paying closer attention to what I had asked. Suddenly the answers began flowing.

Soon afterward, I faced my next challenge—a situation that needed a "mountain moving" prayer. Of course, it was not a literal mountain, but it felt like one when I learned that a story I had written on a professional athlete was in jeopardy because his agent said it would interfere with a book deal. Being a nominal sports fan, I had been in well over my head from the start when I sat in the locker room before the interview. It had been nearly comical, me peering at numbers on jerseys, trying to blend in, pretending I knew the names of the ballplayers every ten-year-old boy can recite like the alphabet. Now I was way out of my league again. I had never met a sports agent, much less known a wheeler-dealer who inked multimillion-dollar contracts.

As I sat understanding my powerlessness, worrying over this immovable mountain, I recalled that Jesus says, "If you have faith as small as a mustard seed you can say to this mountain, 'Move from here to there' and it will move. Nothing will be impossible for you" (Matt. 17:20). *That's the perfect analogy,* I thought, *Here I sit, two thousand years later, understanding exactly the impossibility and improbability of mountains moving.*

There was only one thing to do. I called my favorite "mountain mover," Cathy Belatti, and we agreed to exchange prayers for each other—she for my story permission problem, me for the major sponsor she was trying to land for Women Build for Habitat for Humanity, the volunteer organization that works to eliminate poverty housing.

Then I sat down thinking, *Who do I know nearby who is from the same faith background as this ballplayer who can sit down with me and pray with me about it?* Pam came right to mind, the neighbor I had been reluctant to pray with in chapter 5. The next thing I knew, she had said yes, she would be happy to pray for me, and I was sitting at Pam's kitchen table with my eyes closed in prayer once again.

As all of this praying was going on, something else unusual began happening. I began having dreams at night that helped me better understand myself. Then I started getting outlandish ideas, including a detailed plan for a "surprisedbyprayer.com" web site. Next I had an entire outline for a "100 Answered Prayers" experimental study that would start with a blanket invitation to every house in the neighborhood where I walked. I noted, "I'm amazed at these detailed plans swimming to the surface. It's like prayer is doing a mental housecleaning, and my mind is starting to become uncluttered."

On day nine, as I worried over the still stationary mountain, I received an e-mail from Cathy. She explained that she had gone to church, and as she was praying, she had been startled by a vision. In the vision she saw a desk by a multi-paned window. She wrote, "Beyond the window it was green and sunny, and on the desk was a blue folder, and there were rose petals on the folder. The petals were light colored, white or pale pink. As I prayed I saw drops of blood fall on the folder. It was incredible and very certain. The vision just came to me. I was not expecting or looking for one. I remember sometimes I would pray for a vision and not get one. This time it was clear, and the sense was it was all good."

As I got my bearings back after Cathy's astonishing vision, I counted it as answer number twenty-six, unique in many ways. Even though it was wordless, it conveyed encouragement to me to keep praying because God was working in unseen ways. It also strengthened Cathy as she experienced that extraordinary moment of God's presence. And in the overall scheme of my prayer experiment, it introduced me to an awestruck moment when all powers of human reasoning fall limply by the wayside.

Since I did not send the story off in a blue folder, I began wondering furiously, *Did the sports agent put the story into a blue folder? On the other hand, if it was not literal, what might it mean figuratively? And what of the sunshine, the desk, the rose petals, the blood?* Finally I accepted the fact that I might never know precisely. And in that moment of accepting my imprecise knowledge, I finally accepted a small glimpse of the gigantic mystery of prayer.

Prayer answers number twenty-eight and twenty-nine brought me right back down to earth. Both were "no" concerning projects that I had worked on half a year earlier. I rested the point of my pen on the page, wondering whether I should put these rejections on the list. Finally I decided, *Count them as you would count any other event. They may not be pleasant or welcomed, but they are replies nevertheless.*

Just as I mentioned to God how depressed and let down I was feeling, the words to a song we sing in church came into my mind about how God can make a way when there seems no way out. Suddenly I felt reassured and comforted, even though my circumstances had not changed. I still did not know how I was going to proceed, but at least I knew who would be with me in the meantime. I wrote down, "This is answer to prayer number thirty, because God just reminded me of his presence through remembered words to a song."

On day twelve of the experiment, I stumbled onto my most memorable failure. That morning when I went to tell Gordon good-bye, I said, "Good luck on your presentation," ignoring the impulse to say, *I'll be praying for you.* I let it die before saying it because I felt this praying thing was getting a bit stale and repetitious. And did I need to bother God every time Gordon had another presentation? I mean, could every presentation be *that* important?

Strike two came later, on my morning walk. I have a waving relationship with the high school bus driver, and for the first time I can remember, I arrived at a stop just as the door was open to let on students. The thought came, *You should poke your head in the bus door and tell the driver you pray for her every day when you wave.* Again I drew back, thinking, *That's a bit much, and would I even be able to speak loud enough for her to hear me with all of those kids on the bus?* I silently waved and walked on. The same scene repeated itself at the next major intersection with the middle school bus—the same waving relationship, the same open door, the same pesky thought to say, *I pray for you when I wave,* the same, *No way I'm going to say that,* the same silent wave as I passed.

I was just walking around what I have since named "confession curve," that last curve right before my house where God starts to mention things we need to discuss. As I rounded the bend, I suddenly added up my strikes—one with Gordon, two with the bus drivers. I realized that I had earned what I call the "Perfect Peter Score," after Simon Peter, who denied Christ three times (John 18:17, 25, 27). It was not even eight o'clock in the morning, and like Peter, I was already 0-for-3. I found myself praying a humble prayer of repentance, followed by, "Lord, next time help me to speak up."

At 7:25 that evening, I was in an elementary school cafeteria at a pizza fund-raiser along with 350 parents and hyperactive children packed in so tightly you could hardly pull back your chair. On the far side of the room I glimpsed a woman from church and remembered, *For some reason, she came into your mind this week and you prayed for her.* This time instead of fighting the thought, I fought my way across the room and told her, "I just wanted to let you know that I'd been praying for you this week. I don't know why. You just came to my mind."

A look of incredible relief crossed the woman's face as she said, "Thanks so much! I've had a really tough week. I felt like breaking down and crying over the smallest things." She went on to tell me that she always suffered from depression at this time of year, but never would have admitted it before. I gave her a hug, and we had a meaningful conversation right there in that chaotic cafeteria.

When I took my seat, I barely noticed that the child across the table was swinging her legs and kicking my shins, because I was finally back where I was supposed to be, having been served answer to prayer number thirty-seven and God's presence, along with a slice of pizza on a paper plate. In that small hug, both my friend and I had found God when we each needed him. I smiled and finished my pizza, glad that as long as there is prayer, you never have to leave a "Perfect Peter Score" up in lights, but instead you can get right back into the game.

After two-and-a-half weeks, I skimmed back over my writings and found that I had already written eighty-two pages in my journal. I reflected on what I was learning and wrote, "In the past when I looked for answers to prayer, I always mentally inserted the word *resolution* for *answer*. But I'm seeing that *answer* can also mean *reply*. Reply means a dialogue is going on. No wonder I wasn't getting many prayer answers before, because I was only counting final resolutions and not counting progress, plans, ideas, encouragement, and strength I was getting along the way."

Answer to prayer number forty-two was right before my eyes, and that is why I nearly missed it. I was reviewing John's weekly school papers and as usual, his teacher had drawn a big S, for satisfactory, over the entire area where she can comment on work habits and discipline.

For the first time, I connected the big S to a small prayer that John repeats every night when we tuck him into bed. Without stopping to breathe, he rattles off a prayer for his two older brothers and himself, "Please help Jeff do good in school, please help Chris do good in school, help me do good in school." In fact, the prayer is so much like a prerecorded message in his head, we often laugh in the middle of the summer when no one is in school and the "do good in school" prayer starts spewing from John's mouth.

There that large "Satisfactory" was again, coming home as it always did every Friday in John's book bag, an answer to prayer right before my eyes all along, and this was the very first time I had seen it. I signed my name in the folder, then I signed into my journal and wrote down answer number forty-two—presence—because every night John prayed about school, and every day God sat down at the desk with him the next morning.

The "do good in school" answer got me to thinking about other routine prayers about daily safety. I wrote, "I was

245

wondering why I wasn't finding more dazzling instances of presence, but now I see that it comes every day in the form of personal safety. I've been doing this experiment for seventeen days. What if I went back and added up all five of our family members who have enjoyed daily safety during that time? I'd have eighty-five answers of presence and help."

Fourteen days after I had enlisted help with my "mountain moving prayer," the mountain finally gave up and moved. When I received word that the ballplayer in question had finally faxed in his signature on the piece, I nearly laughed out loud trying to figure what a mountain really would look like in the act of moving. In my imagination it scooted over just a little, like a bucket full of wet beach sand. Whatever the case, God had changed the mind of a hard-nosed professional sports agent and had landed the permission of a multimillion-dollar big-league player!

While I was still congratulating myself over this stunning answer, the chairman of a local chapter of a club whose speaking circuits I travel called about the upcoming meeting at which I would be the guest speaker. "We're praying to have eighty women there," she said.

I answered breezily, "Good. I'll pray, too."

Then she said, "I sent you extra invitations in case you could bring someone you know who hasn't heard you speak."

This time, no "good" came out of my mouth. It was more like a gulp. Of course I had plenty of friends I might invite, but the whole idea was to invite people who might not be able to go to church regularly but who might accept an invitation to a luncheon.

I hung up the phone realizing one of the dangers of my prayer experiment: the danger of using prayer as an excuse not to get to work, the danger of pretending that I had done my whole duty once the praying was over. God, on the other hand, was setting up an experiment of his own. If I did not mind *praying* that eighty women would come, would I mind *inviting* women to reach that goal?

I said, "Well, God, if you want me to ask someone, who?" The name of a neighbor came straight into my mind, one whose house I passed daily, saying that nice prayer about churches and growing in faith. Suddenly I was in a bigger pickle, because I had duties at the head table, and I could not leave one lonely neighbor sitting out there in a sea of strangers. I finally gave up and decided to invite every woman on my cul-de-sac who was home during the day. I invited nine women. Exactly two could come. Of course, it was no surprise as I listed answer to prayer number forty-nine that of the two who accepted, one was the woman whose name had dropped into my mind. In the past when I had heard someone say he or she was "putting feet under my prayers" by going out after what they wanted, I had secretly thought it an excuse not to wait for God. But prayer answer number forty-nine taught me the dangers of hiding behind any excuses, worldly or pious, in our pursuit of answers to prayer.

On day twenty-six, we got an e-mail from our son Chris, off at college in California, saying that he felt he had done well on his midterms. I wondered, *Is this worth recording since I've recorded other good test results?* I reflected in my journal, "This isn't just an exam for Chris, it's a checkup on my willingness to identify prayer answers, no matter how repetitious. The only reason I wasn't going to put it down was the good old American idea that things have to be novel, new, unusual, and colossal to be noteworthy. If I felt even a small thankfulness to God, I should count it, even though it might not make front page news at the next prayer meeting." And so I dutifully recorded answer number sixty-one.

On day twenty-six, we were in the minivan ready to pull out for a short weekend getaway, and without my knowing it, this break in the routine had unconsciously caused me to drift away from prayer. Then John piped up from the backseat, "We forgot to say a prayer for safety." We bowed our heads and said a quick prayer.

The next day we were enjoying a pleasant winter ride atop a twenty-mile-long ridge at Roosevelt State Park where the spine of the mountain is just wide enough for the two-lane road. Our son Jeff was driving around fifty miles an hour when I suddenly saw two deer jumping up on the left side of the ridge, ready to bound in front of us. "Jeff, deer!" I yelled. He never saw the deer, but he reacted to my words and hit the brakes. The first deer bounded in front of our car and disappeared with a flash of a white tail over the ridge. The second deer froze like a statue instead of crossing the road and then bolted off in the direction he had come.

"Thanks for the warning," Jeff said. "If I hadn't slowed or if that second deer hadn't stopped, we definitely would have hit one or the other." As I wrote down answer to prayer number sixty-two, I was thankful to God not only for safety but also that he never takes a vacation on his end of the prayer line.

The most unusual call to pray came while I was reading the newspaper and shaking my head over the latest violence in the Middle East. A thought strayed into my mind about praying, but I figured, *Why waste my time? Problems have been going on in the Middle East since before I was born, and it's never going to get any better.* Then an answering thought came just as clearly as my own thought before it, *Yes, but it says in the Bible to pray for the peace of Jerusalem* (Ps. 122:6).

A few days later, I told God how worried I was that time was running out and I really needed to get in touch with Jama Hedgecoth, whose story about Spirit is in chapter 7. I called again, and her answering machine kicked in. I spoke a long monologue into the machine about what I wanted to do, the sooner the better. I was so busy trying to think if I had missed saying something that when I went to end the message, I accidentally said, "Have a great day, and amen."

I started laughing right on Jama's answering machine and tried again. "I meant to say good-bye. Oh, well!" *Karen*, I thought, *you're so far gone on this prayer experiment, now you're saying amen to answering machines!*

I realized how tense I had been, and the laughter felt ever so good because it was loosening something up inside of me and I could feel the stress shriveling. I had certainly ended that message in an offbeat way, but I suddenly realized that God was coming to my aid in one of his more offbeat ways through the gift of a good, hearty laugh. I wrote down answer number seventy, glad that God was smart enough to invent humor.

The events of answer number seventy-two started rolling as I drove to South Carolina to meet my father and my sister Susan for a visit in a small tourist town. As I drove, I was thinking about what to do with a check I had just received, and the thought came to my mind, *Give unto the* LORD *the first fruits of thy labor* (Leviticus 23:9–14). By this time in the experiment I was familiar with where those out-of-the-blue thoughts were always headed, so I said back, "What do you mean 'first fruits'? I've been writing for twenty years."

The thought came back, *In Leviticus it talks about fruit trees when the Israelites were commanded not to eat the fruit of each tree until the fifth year and from then on, it was theirs. This is about the first fruits of your latest project* (Lev. 19:23–25).

Now, that Scripture coming to my mind makes me out to be more of a Bible scholar than I am. The truth is, I often recall snippets of Scripture, but I have to search a concordance to find where they are in the Bible so I can read what they actually say. The only reason this Old Testament verse was in my memory bank was because I had studied it closely several years earlier when my life was on hold and I was unearthing any and every formula about God's timing, likely or unlikely, including those about fruit trees.

"All right, God," I prayed. "If you want me to give away this check, help me get on board with this idea."

The next day as Dad and Susan and I were strolling down Main Street in the small town, Dad noticed a sign outside a church with the name of a minister he had known years earlier. "Oh, do we have time tomorrow before leaving to go to church?" he asked. "Of course," I said, biting my tongue over the fact that I had not given any thought to going to church and had not even packed a skirt.

So there I sat on Sunday morning in a church I had not dreamed of going to, hiding on a back pew in a pair of slacks. Since at our church back home we always write a check beforehand for the collection, I found myself going for my wallet for the first time in years, for something to toss politely into the plate. I was relieved to come up with two one-dollar bills. But as I pulled them out, I noticed that someone had written a message all around the border of one of the bills. *What in the world?* I thought. *You'd think I would have noticed all of these markings when someone gave me this bill in change.* I sat there turning the bill all around, straining to read the tiny writing. This is what it said: "Give this money away and you will be blessed. I love you." *What a strange coincidence that this bill shows up in my hand right when there's a collection plate in front of me and not when I'm standing at a cash register somewhere. I think I'm on board now, God, about our little chat about generosity.*

I put the bill into the plate, wondering how many times the church treasurer had seen it recycled in the small town.

On March 13, fifty-one days after I began my experiment and after 208 journal pages, I wrote down answer number one hundred. And what sort of grand finale did God have planned for me? Something dramatic and glorious? No. He sent a bumper sticker. There I was pulling up the interstate exit ramp thinking, *I've been working so hard. I deserve a break. Lord, I think I'll just drop by the antique store and browse instead of hurrying back to work.* And there, just in front of me, happened to be a bumper sticker on the back window of car where van drivers like myself would be sure to see it. It read, "W.W.J.D." and in smaller letters said, "What would Jesus do?"

I was familiar with the bracelets that people wear to remind themselves of that question in their daily actions, but I had always thought it applied to moral decisions and treating others fairly. I had never thought about applying it to decisions about whether to fritter away some time in an antique store or to get right back to work. *I know exactly what Jesus would do,* I thought. *He'd go home and get back to work.* And so I did. I went home and got back to the work of recording answer to prayer number one hundred, beginning the entry, "Well, I knew a bumper sticker would get worked in sooner or later."

Several days after the one-hundredth prayer answer, I was approaching an intersection on my morning walk and saw the middle-school bus stopping to open the door just ahead. Instead of dragging my feet, I picked up my pace, thinking, *What an opportunity!* It felt like forever between my last step and the lingering open door as the very last student found a seat in the back. I poked in my head and waved my hand and said to the bus driver, "May God bless you today!" The woman's face let out a grin, and she nodded back pleasantly. As I walked around confession curve, I was nearly in tears I was so happy.

My prayer experiment had turned out to be the experience of a lifetime. Through looking for prayer answers, I had found myself suddenly in the middle of paradise, strewn with favors from God. Here there were no moments in life that did not matter, no people who should forever remain strangers, no times of utter aloneness. I had indeed found my own small heaven here on earth, and it was all because my life had been completely and forever surprised by the transforming power of prayer.

Time to Ask

We have been conversing now for eight chapters on how we are often surprised by prayer, and it's here at the conclusion that we will turn the tables and consider the times that Jesus himself was surprised. If we had been in his place, surely we would have been surprised by the wind and waves obeying our will, a dead man rising up still bound in the grave clothes, a paralyzed man walking, a blind man seeing. Yet none of the gospel writers record any degree of surprise in Jesus when these astounding things happened. Instead Mark says of Jesus, "And he was amazed at their lack of faith" (Mark 6:6). It is our lack of prayer and our lack of expectation that makes us completely astonishing creatures to our Lord and the hosts of angels.

Saint Paul says, "Do not be anxious about anything, but in everything by prayers and petitions, with thanksgiving, present your requests to God. And the peace of God, which transcends all understanding, will guard your hearts and your minds in Christ Jesus" (Phil. 4:6–7).

In this verse, Paul gives us a simple test for those subjects that are permissible for petition. He does not categorize things into big or small, worthy or selfish, holy or mundane. His only guideline is that the subject of our petitions be something or anything that makes us anxious or worried.

Paul goes on to explain the precise reward in petitioning God about such things. We are not promised that we will receive the outcomes we are imagining. Instead, we shall discover a peace that transcends events and situations. We shall have a new guard for our hearts and minds—the assurance that God is there.

Paul links petition with thanksgiving. Faith is directional. Our need brings us to call upon God. God answers. We thank him for this particular help. The particular help causes us to wonder about the God who sent it. We move from the particular answer to the general feeling that God is big and gracious and vast, too big for us to see, yet small enough to know us. And so petition and faith lap against the shore, rolling from the particular to the general and from the general back to the particular again, all the while filling our souls with the soothing certainty of the God who is there. For there is nothing more exhilarating than becoming faith experimenters, riding the waves of surprise back and forth in the mysterious realm of prayer.

During this investigation we have found that prayer answers come in all sizes, covering the whole spectrum of life experiences from natural to other-earthly, from mundane to spectacular, from laughable to laudable, from faint whispers to unmistakable shouts. Our challenge is to see and count the natural, the mundane, the laughable, and the whisperings as "just perfect" and just as perfectly divine. Once we begin collecting all shapes and sizes of prayer answers into our souls, we will never be strengthless or alone.

Surprised by an Opening Prayer

Often when we part from a gathering, we bow our heads in a closing prayer. Here at the end of our journey, let us do something unpredictable and share an opening prayer. It is an opening prayer, not because it precedes something, but rather because it looses power as it opens our hearts and minds to the delightful answers that God is ready to send our way the minute we bow our heads.

Dear Lord,
Today as I bring my needs to you,
I also pray that you will fill my greater need
To be open to the possibilities of your answers.
Help me to accept unlikely means,
In the same way you accepted me when least likely to succeed.
As I pray for rescue,
Rescue me from forgetting that you are always there.
As I search for answers,
Help me listen for your words
And lead me to follow your directions.
May I respond to calls to pray,
Trusting you will supply the words.
Open me to accept new partnerships,
To broaden my faith and narrow my faults.
Help me diligently store the Scriptures,
So they might answer me with truth.
May I never stop being amazed by your answers
So that I might stand daily in awe
Applauding the ways you are at work in my life.
Today and forever may I always be
Surprised by prayer.

Karen Barber is a contributing editor with *Guideposts* magazine, and her works appear in the yearly devotional book *Daily Guideposts*. She is the author of *Ready, Set . . . Wait*, which offers help for those going through waiting periods in life. Karen is a popular inspirational speaker who is currently developing a video series about interactive prayer called *Personal Prayer Power*.

At the conclusion of *Surprising Ways God Answers Prayer*, Karen began an experiment to record 100 personal answers to prayer. After successfully finding 100 answers, she decided to continue the practice and now has over 1,000 answers to prayer written in her journal.

Karen and her husband, Gordon, have three sons, Jeff, Chris, and John, and live in Alpharetta, Georgia.

If you'd like to share a prayer request or answer to prayer or contact Karen, visit www.surprisedbyprayer.com.